Aug	Mercenaries enter Guatemala City and massacre Arbenz supporters; Ernesto flees to the Argentinian Embassy.
21st Sept	Ernesto reaches Mexico City and finds work as a doctor.

★ 1955

15th May	Fidel Castro and other Moncadistas freed from prison in Cuba.
June	Ñico López organizes a meeting between Ernesto and Raúl Castro.
7th July	Fidel Castro arrives in Mexico, aiming to prepare an armed invasion of Cuba.
July	Ernesto meets Fidel Castro and joins his group of trainee guerrilla fighters as their doctor; he becomes known as "Che."
18th Aug	Ernesto marries Hilda Gadea, a Peruvian political activist he met in Guatemala.

★ 1956

15th Feb	Ernesto and Hilda's child, Hilda Beatriz Guevara, is born.
24th June	Che, Fidel Castro, and 26 other members of the group are arrested and held in detention under immigration laws, Che for 57 days.
25th Nov	Che is among the 82 fighters who sail from Tuxpán, Mexico, for Cuba aboard the yacht *Granma*.
2nd Dec	The *Granma* reaches Las Coloradas beach in south eastern Cuba.

	...); ...ed, and Che is wounded and separated from Castro's group.
21st Dec	Che is reunited with Castro's group, which is reduced to 15 rebels.

★ 1957

17th Jan	Rebel Army takes an army position at La Plata.
28th May	Rebel Army captures a well fortified garrison at El Uvero in the Sierra Maestra.
July	A second column is created under the leadership of Che, who is promoted to Comandante.

★ 1958

July	Rebel Army defeats Batista's forces at El Jigüe and moves onto the offensive.
31st Aug	Che sets out with a column for Las Villas province in central Cuba.
16th Oct	Che's column reaches the Escambray Mountains.
28th Dec	Che launches the battle for Santa Clara, capital of Las Villas.

★ 1959

1st Jan	Batista flees Cuba as Santa Clara falls and Che sets out for Havana.
2nd Jan	The country is paralyzed by a general strike called by Castro.
3rd Jan	Che reaches Havana and occupies the Cabaña fortress.

the
Che
handbook

Above: **RAFAEL ENRÍQUEZ, 1987**

the
Che
handbook

Hilda Barrio
Gareth Jenkins
Interviews by Andrés Castillo Bernal

ST. MARTIN'S PRESS 🙢 NEW YORK

Che comand

ante, amigo

Acknowledgments

Many people offered their whole-hearted support in the preparation of this book. We thank them every one, even though space does not permit us to name them all. We specially wish to thank:

Zaro Weil, whose idea it was to create this book, for her judgment and support throughout and in giving it its final form.

The Office of Historical Affairs of Cuba's Council of State for making its photographic and documentary archive available, and specially Efrén González for his acute advice and extraordinary patience with two authors who knew much less about Che than he did.

Andrés Castillo for his passion, and for his skill in undertaking the interviews for the book.

The friends of Che who agreed to provide their recollections of the man they so admired—Alberto Granado, Víctor Dreke, Oscar Fernández Mell, Ulises Estrada, and Alberto Castellanos.

The Che Guevara Center in Havana, and particularly Aleida March, Camilo Guevara, and María del Carmen Ariett for their invaluable cooperation.

The photographers Perfecto Romero, Liborio Noval, Chino López, Sergio Romero, Lisette Solorzano, Keith Cardwell, and all the anonymous photographers who have created such a remarkable visual record of Che and the events he lived through.

Mirtha Ibarra y José Angel Toirac for their unconditional support.

Guillermo Bello for his professional restoration of all the images.

The graphic propaganda office of the Department of Revolutionary Orientation, the Organization for Solidarity with the Peoples of Asia, Africa and Latin America (OSPAAAL), and the photographic department of Prensa Latina.

All the designers and painters who over the years have made their own testimony to Che through their art.

The team at MQ Publications in London, who consistently produce such beautiful books.

Steve Wilkinson for his generous advice.

Preface

Ernesto Guevara, later to become known the world over as Che, was born in Argentina in 1928. He was 8 years old when the Spanish Civil War began, and eleven at the outbreak of the Second World War.

Che's student years coincided with a period when strong nationalist and left-wing political movements were emerging in Argentina and throughout Latin America. This was also the period when armed struggles for independence were emerging in the colonies and semi-colonies of Africa and Asia.

After university, and until his death in 1967 in Bolivia, where he was leading a guerrilla campaign, Che devoted himself to political and economic independence for the countries of "Our America" and the other countries of what became known as the Third World.

In Mexico in 1956 Che joined a small group of Cubans under the leadership of Fidel Castro to launch an invasion of Cuba. They waged a guerrilla campaign that, two years later, was instrumental in the overthrow of the government of Fulgencio Batista.

Cuba is the largest island in the Caribbean, and at that time had a population of 5 million. It shared its colonial past with the rest of Latin America, and had only won independence from Spain in 1898. But it had never enjoyed full political independence, since soon after it became a semi-colonial protectorate of the United States. By the 1950s the Cuban economy was dominated by large US corporations and US mafia bosses, to whom the government was beholden.

A number of political movements emerged to challenge the corruption of the Batista regime. The most audacious of these was the 26th July Movement, inspired by the 1953 attack on the Moncada Barracks in Santiago de Cuba by a group led by Fidel Castro.

Note: All quotations are from Che Guevara, unless otherwise indicated.

Following page: **RAFAEL ENRÍQUEZ**

Passion is needed for any great work, and for the Revolution passion and audacity are required in big doses

8 OCTUBRE · OCTOBER 8 · 8 OCTOBRE · ٨ اكتوبر

Día del Guerrillero Heroico · Journée du Guerrillero Héroïque

Day of the Heroic Guerrilla · يوم المجاهد البطل

Introduction

Barely a year ago, by one of those coincidences of fate, the idea emerged among a group of friends to produce a book about Che. It would be a book which would open up for young people the life and thinking of this exceptional man, who was in turn Ernesto Guevara, Tete, Tatu, Ramón … and the legendary guerrilla known the world over as Che.

I never met Che, but I have the privilege to belong to a generation full of dreams, a generation that was prepared to make a sacrifice doing the voluntary work that Che advocated. We did not hesitate to accept moral incentives in place of material rewards, working to create the New Man that Che exhorted us to create. We learned to love Che, sharing his thinking as something everyday.

For the next generations Che, transformed into the image of the guerrilla, became something different. Some took up his ideas and turned them into slogans, others seized on him as a symbol of political and social revolt.

If one is to discover the man behind the symbol, the photographic record is only part of the story. To expand on it we have selected passages from Che's speeches, diaries, poems, essays, and letters which show the sharpness and depth of his thinking, and which provide a testimony to his place in history.

This exceptional man knew how to use his intelligence and judgment all the circumstances he encountered, taking advantage of each moment as if it were the last sip of the *mate* infusion he was devoted to. The life he chose offered him the chance to decide his destiny, and he embraced this challenge with all his passion.

Hilda Barrio
Havana, May 2003

I first visited Cuba in 1987, 20 years after the death of Che Guevara in Bolivia. I suppose I must have expected to find Che commemorated in the country he dedicated himself so passionately to, but I was not prepared to find him so much alive in the hearts of the people. I remember feeling quite moved the first time I heard a trio sing Carlos Puebla's song "Comandante Che Guevara," moved because the people around me were so moved.

Over the years I occasionally read writings by or about Che, but never in a very focused way. I knew that he had been an exceptional guerrilla fighter, and wholly dedicated to the cause of political and economic independence for Latin America. But what his contribution had been, I wasn't quite sure.

When I found myself swept up in the project to write this book I buried myself in Che's own writings. It was a humbling experience to recognize the determination with which he directed his considerable energies towards his goals. He saw politics and armed struggle as the means to improve life for ordinary people, and he believed that US imperialism posed the greatest threat to the peace and prosperity of the poor countries of the world.

Che often called himself a dreamer, but one who fought to turn his dreams into reality. He had a hunger for practical detail and a readiness to learn whatever was necessary. As a guerrilla fighter, as a roving ambassador after Cuba's 1959 Revolution, or as president of Cuba's national bank, he was single-minded and consistent in everything he did. That is what won him the devotion of those who knew him, and the admiration of those who did not.

Gareth Jenkins
London, May 2003

★ Early years

This haphazard traveling through our Greater America has changed me more than I realized

Che Guevara was born Ernesto Guevara de la Serna on 14th June 1928, in Rosario, north-east of the Argentinian capital, Buenos Aires. He acquired the nickname "Che" many years later from his Cuban comrades.

Both his father, **Ernesto Guevara Lynch**, and his mother, **Celia de la Serna**, came from established Argentinian families with connections among the ruling classes. But both were socially non-conformist and politically radical, and they brought up their five children, of whom Ernesto was the eldest, to be open-minded and questioning.

Ernesto senior tried his hand at a variety of business enterprises. He started a plantation to grow yerba mate, a type of green tea which is the national drink of Argentina; he became involved in boat building; and later he worked as an architect and building contractor. But he seems not to have had a real taste for business, and the family fortunes were often precarious.

Ernesto's mother Celia was strong-willed and passionate about ideas, and particularly about French culture. She had met her husband at university and they filled their house with books, artists, bohemians, and intellectuals.

At the age of two Ernesto developed **severe asthma** which was to dog him for the rest of his life. His parents' efforts to alleviate it came to dominate the life of the family, eventually dictating their move to Alta Gracia in Córdoba province in search of dry air and an equable climate. Ernesto's father encouraged him to take up

sports, which he did with a passion. During his childhood and early youth he became accomplished at swimming, horse riding, soccer, rugby, table tennis, shooting, flying planes, and golf. He also became an outstanding **chess** player.

Ernesto's struggle to overcome his asthma developed in him an extraordinary **will power** and a sense of **purpose**. Even so, there were long periods when he was unable to attend school, and his mother taught him his lessons at home. He read voraciously and widely, choosing books well in advance of his years. His mother also taught him French, and by the time he reached the age of 12 he was already reading French poetry in the original language.

Ernesto grew up hearing political discussion and debate in the house. When he was nine his parents set up a support committee for Spanish Republicans who had come to Argentina fleeing from the Spanish Civil War. His mother's elder sister was married to a communist poet and journalist who went to Spain to cover the war on behalf of a pro-Republican Argentine paper, and the family used to read aloud the regular despatches he sent back home. This must have made a significant impression on the young Ernesto, but he was not to display a strong interest in politics until he went to university.

By the time Ernesto began his studies at the **University** of Buenos Aires in 1946, the family was back living in the capital. He chose medicine for his degree course.

As a young man Ernesto developed **a thirst for adventure**, which increasingly became fuelled by a desire to understand the social conditions of the poor of Latin America. In 1950 he added a motor to his bicycle and set off on a 3,000-mile tour of Argentina, meeting up with his great friend Alberto Granado on the way. The following year he took a job as a nurse on a cargo ship and sailed around Latin America.

Later that year Ernesto and Alberto Granado made a trip around **South America** that for Ernesto was to last nine months, on a 500cc Norton motor bike they named *La Poderosa* ("the Powerful One"). They set out in December 1951, but had to abandon the bike when it broke down and continue by hitching.

In **Chile** Ernesto was shocked by the conditions he found on a visit to the copper mine Chuquicamata. He found the peasants and the workers hopelessly poor and exploited. One night they made friends with Chilean workers who were communists who had been imprisoned following the uprising of 1948:

> **We made friends with a Chilean worker couple who were communists... The couple, numb with cold, huddling together in the desert night ... They didn't have a single miserable blanket to sleep under, so we gave them one of ours and Alberto and I wrapped the other one round us as best we could. It was one of the coldest experiences I have ever had; but also one which made me feel a little closer to this strange, for me, human species.**

In **Peru** he was overwhelmed by the remains of the ancient civilization of the Incas at the mountain-top city of Machu Picchu, and developed a fascination for **archeology** which stayed with him all his life.

The two travelers worked in a leper colony in Peru, then moved on to Bogotá, **Colombia**, where civil war still smoldered following the uprising of 1948. When they reached Caracas, **Venezuela**, Alberto stayed to work in a laboratory, while Ernesto flew to **Miami** and from there back to Buenos Aires to take his final medical exams.

The experience of traveling with very little money, and taking jobs along the way, brought Ernesto into close contact with the peoples of the South American continent and forged his belief in the goal of a united America. Throughout the trip he kept a **diary** of his impressions, as he was to do for the rest of his life.

This journey has only served to confirm this belief, that the division of America into unstable and illusory nations is a complete fiction. We are one single mestizo race with remarkable ethnographical similarities, from Mexico down to the Magellan Straits.

Above left: **First born, Palermo, Argentina, July 1928**
Barely one month old, Ernesto Guevara de la Serna is held by his
mother, Celia.

Above right: **"Tete," Galarza, Argentina, 1929**
Ernesto's parents affectionately called him "Tete," the first of
many nicknames and pseudonyms that he was to acquire.

Right: **Celia and "Tete," Buenos Aires, 1929**
A particularly strong relationship developed between Celia and
Ernesto. Their closeness is evident in many of the letters Ernesto
wrote to his mother. Celia was a woman of strong character who
read widely and was constantly inviting artists and intellectuals to
the house. Her political views became increasingly radical with
the years, in sympathy with those of her eldest son.

I never got used to hearing him breathe with that particular sound

Recollection of Ernesto Guevara senior

Above: **With his cousins, Asochinga, Córdoba, Argentina, 1931**

Ernesto (center) grew up surrounded by love, with strong family ties and a full social life in the company of aunts and uncles, cousins and friends.

Left: **In Morón, Buenos Aires, Argentina, 1930**

Ernesto was just two years old when he first began to suffer from asthma attacks. This illness was to remain with him for the rest of his life, and his efforts to overcome it helped shape his remarkably determined character.

Left: **In Alta Gracia with his parents, Córdoba, Argentina, 1934**

Ernesto's asthma attacks became so severe that they influenced the life of the whole family. In 1932, when he was four, the family moved to Alta Gracia, a spa town with a dry climate in the central highlands of Córdoba province which offered relief for people suffering from respiratory ailments. They were to live there for the next 11 years.

His parents took great care of him and during the periods when he was confined at home because of his asthma his mother spent hours nursing him and teaching him. Despite his asthma Ernesto developed a taste for rough play, a disheveled appearance, and breaking the rules. There was always a group of kids around him ready for mischief.

Left: **In Alta Gracia, Córdoba, Argentina, 1933**

Ernesto is dressed in his riding clothes ready to ride his pet mule. His father imbued all his children with a love of sport and a thirst for adventure.

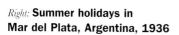

Right: **Summer holidays in Mar del Plata, Argentina, 1936**

Although the family's fortunes were precarious throughout Ernesto's childhood, they lived a normal middle-class life. They often took their holidays in Mar del Plata, Argentina's most popular summer resort. These were difficult periods for Ernesto since cold water frequently triggered his asthma attacks.

Above: **With his sister Ana María, Alta Gracia, Argentina, 1940**

Right: **Negrina, Alta Gracia, Córdoba, Argentina, 1939**
Ernesto with his brother Roberto and sisters Ana María and
Celia, together with Negrina, the family's dog.

The smallest children would spend all day playing with her: they would pull her ears, curl her whiskers or roll around on the floor with her. Negrina grew up like a brute, enjoying the wild ways of my children.

Recollection of Ernesto Guevara senior

You were always an apostolic and evangelical adventurer, as well as an athletic and brave boy who knew how to turn a somersault and land in the same spot

León Felipe, *Poems to Che*

Left: **The family, Mar del Plata, Argentina, 1943**

Celia, Celia de la Serna, Roberto, Ana Maria, and Ernesto, with Juan being held by his father.

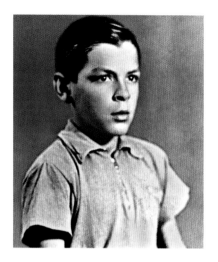

Left: **Alta Gracia, Argentina, 1940**

During this period Ernesto developed an enthusiasm for chess, which became a lifelong passion.

Left: **Córdoba, Argentina, 1944**

The family's move to Córdoba when he was 15 initiated a period when Ernesto made strong friendships and his love of reading developed. He also took up rugby, and was coached by Alberto Granado who was to become a lifelong friend.

Left: **Buenos Aires, Argentina, 1948**

Ernesto's reputation for high spirits, independence, and disregard for danger carried through into his student years. At this time his parents separated, the family once again faced difficult financial problems and he took a number of odd jobs to earn money. He had a reputation among his friends for being fun-loving and adventurous.

He looked and acted much older than he was and was clearly already grown up with a definite personality

Recollection of Che's teacher, Alfredo Pueyredon

Che on travel
I now know by an unbelievable coincidence of fate that I am destined to travel

Left: **The wanderer, Argentina, 1948**
After taking his medical exams in December Ernesto made several trips rather than staying in Buenos Aires retaking exams. He traveled all over Santa Fe as well as north from Córdoba and east from Mendoza. He was more interested in studying what would be useful than what would get him a good qualification.

Right: **Exploring Argentina, Córdoba, 1950**
Almost unrecognizable in his traveler's outfit Ernesto—nicknamed "Pelón" by his friends for his unfashionably short hair cut—made long trips on his motorized bicycle into the heartlands of Argentina.

★ Studying to be a doctor

I was restless, in need of satisfying my dreaming spirit; I was fed up with medical school, hospitals, and exams

Ernesto entered the **University of Buenos Aires** in 1946 to study medicine. His decision seems to have been prompted by the experience of nursing his grandmother for the last two weeks of her life.

He was also no doubt influenced in his choice by a desire to understand his own poor health, and he developed an early interest in allergy research. Years later he wrote that he was motivated by the idea of becoming a famous researcher.

At university Ernesto spent hours in the library reading widely in areas such as philosophy, political history, and psychology. He also developed an important platonic relationship with fellow student, **Bertha Gilda Infante**, known as Tita to her friends.

During his studies he took a variety of **medical jobs** to support himself, including working as a nurse on a cargo ship sailing around South America. For several years he worked as a research assistant in an allergy clinic.

On his first long trip around South America in 1952, Ernesto and his friend, Alberto Granado, worked for a while in a **Peruvian leper colony**. After he graduated he set off on a trip which took him to Guatemala, where he developed the idea of working for two years as a rural doctor and writing a book about the role which doctors could play in supporting revolution in Latin America. Although medicine was not to become his career, it allowed him early contact with ordinary people.

When I began to study medicine most of the concepts I now have as a revolutionary were then absent from my warehouse of ideals. I wanted to be successful, as everyone does. I used to dream of being a famous researcher, of working tirelessly to achieve something that could, decidedly, be placed at the service of mankind, but which was at that time all about personal triumph. I was, as we all are, a product of my environment.

I heard his deep warm voice several times. The irony in it gave him and all the rest of us courage when we faced something that shook even the most unflappable of those future doctors. You could tell he was provincial by his accent. He was a handsome, easygoing boy. His bearing, a mixture of shyness and haughtiness, maybe recklessness, obscured a deep intelligence, an insatiable thirst for understanding, and, far down, an infinite capacity for loving.

Recollection of fellow student, Tita Infante

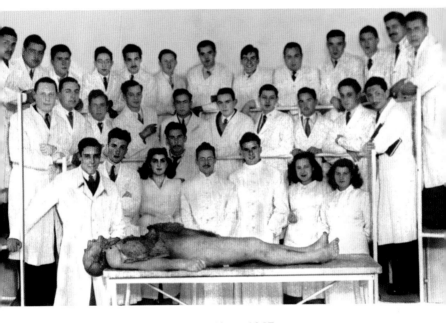

Above: **The Faculty of Medicine, Buenos Aires, 1947**

At the beginning of 1947 Ernesto began his studies at medical school. He is sixth in from the right, top row, with the big smile. Tita Infante is second from right, bottom row.

> **Ernesto was more dynamic and was not bound by the conventional customs that bound the rest of us together ... In his dealings with women he was completely open and that to a certain extent was a source of scandal for their parents.**
>
> **Recollection of a contemporary friend, Fernando Barral**

Above: **With female friends, Argentina, 1948**

Ernesto was attractive to women and had many female admirers.

Above: **Traveling around with friends, Buenos Aires, 1948**

★ Intellectual & artistic studies
He set himself very high standards, something that had shown through from a young age

Recollection of childhood friend, Alberto Granado

Forced by illness to spend long periods at home as a child, and encouraged by his parents, Ernesto became an avid reader. He loved adventure classics, and his complete works of Jules Verne remained one of his most prized possessions later in life. He read popular **modern novels** as well as **classic literature**.

In adolescence he became **passionate about poetry** and he wrote poems throughout his life. His favorite poet was the Chilean Pablo Neruda; a volume of Neruda's poetry was found in his bag after he was killed.

He was an **avid photographer** and spent many hours photographing people and places. In his later travels he enjoyed photographing archeological sites.

As he grew up his interests expanded to include Freud and Bertrand Russell, and everything he could find on **philosophy** from the Ancient Greeks to the present day. He read works by political leaders such as Mussolini, Stalin, and Gandhi and **novelists** such as Emile Zola, Alexandre Dumas, William Faulkner, John Steinbeck, and Jack London. The Indian independence leader Jawaharlal Nehru's *The Discovery of India* impressed him with its ideas about political and economic sovereignty, and fed his growing hostility towards US imperialism.

As a university student Ernesto worked on his own philosophical **notebooks**, cross-referencing and reflecting on everything he read. But, unlike many of his contemporaries, he did not affiliate with any left-wing or nationalist organization at this time. He seems to have decided to think through his experiences and define his own ideas before making any formal commitment.

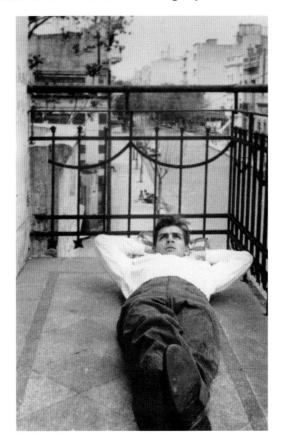

Above: **Daydreaming, Buenos Aires, 1949**
The balcony of Ernesto's room in the family home at 2180 Araoz Street.

In the late afternoon we decided to leave, I on a bicycle, Alberto with a friend on a motor bike

Above: **Inseparable friends, Córdoba, Argentina, 1950**

Ernesto with Tomás and Alberto Granado. He and Alberto shared a thirst for adventure and a desire to see the world, and they became inseparable friends. They were about to set out on a journey of 3,000 miles around Argentina, Ernesto on a motorized bicycle.

After the December examinations, instead of staying in the capital reviewing subjects for the March exams he would put together his knapsack, get on his motorcycle—or sometimes just use his legs—and travel to different parts of the country, both visiting and doing all kinds of odd jobs

Recollection of childhood friend, Alberto Granado

Above: **Getting ready to leave, Córdoba, Argentina, 1951**

During one of his visits to the house of the Granado brothers during the September vacation, Ernesto and Alberto planned their epic trip around South America. Alberto later recalled: " 'Mial ['Mi Alberto'], if you wait until December when I pass my exams, I will accompany you.' And I waited. On 29th December 1951 we mounted a motor bike laden with utensils, shaving soap and other things, including an automatic pistol."

Beneath the vines of Alberto Granado's house we sipped sweet mate and spoke about all the latest events in our "dog's lives," while dedicating ourselves to the task of getting La Poderosa II into shape. He lamented having to abandon his post at the leper colony of San Francisco de Chañar and the miserably paid work at the Spanish hospital. I had also had to abandon my job, but unlike him I was very happy to have done so.

Below: **La Poderosa II, Córdoba, Argentina, October 1951**

The two friends were to set off around South America at the end of the year on their dream machine, *La Poderosa II*, the Powerful One.

Our first experience on unpaved roads was alarming: nine spills in a single day. However, lying on campbeds, the only beds we'd know from now on, beside La Poderosa, our snail-like abode, we looked into the future with impatient joy. We seemed to breathe more freely, a lighter air, an air of adventure. Faraway countries, heroic deeds, beautiful women whirled round and round in our turbulent imaginations.

Interview with Alberto Granado

Above: **Camilo Cienfuegos School, Havana, 1995**
Alberto Granado and Che's daughter Hilda Gadea in front of a
statue of Camilo Cienfuegos, at a memorial ceremony for Che.

**Born in Córdoba, Argentina. Studied biochemistry and traveled with Ernesto
throughout Latin America for the best part of a year. After the Revolution he
went to live in Cuba and worked as a university professor and in research.
He was one of the early initiators of Cuba's biotechnology program.**

Interview in Havana, 23rd December 2002

We always had our own unique understanding of what friendship
meant: that friendship is to be valued above everything else.
Whenever one of our women was unfaithful to us we would say to
each other: "I feel sorry for you, as a friend of mine; not for her as
she's been unfaithful to you."

It wasn't easy to be Ernesto's friend as there's always a little tendency to let a friend get away with a lot more. It's often said of a friend that he's a drunkard, a womanizer or that he treats women with no respect. But a friend is a friend and as such you defend him. Not that Che did any of that. A friend was a friend as long as he acted in the same way that had helped make us friends in the first place—honorable, a good friend, and always prepared to give to those who had nothing.

He was extremely upright and set himself very high standards, something that shone through from a young age. If you couldn't stand criticism, liked flattery, in other words deluded yourself, there wasn't much chance of becoming Che's friend. He was always prepared to go for the jugular and, sooner or later, he would make you angry.

Often when you did him a favor out of kindness, he would respond curtly. There's one story in particular. In 1950 I was working in a leper colony in San Francisco de Chañar and Che, who at the time was studying to be a doctor, was touring Argentina on a motorbike. He was visiting all 14 provinces in the country, a journey of some 3,000 miles, and he stopped by the leper colony to spend some time with me. We repaired his motor bike so that he could go on with his journey and on the day of his departure we organized a party. Some girls who were friends of mine came to the party and we were having a great time. When we got up to get a drink I remembered that he didn't like drinking, just occasionally having a soft drink with ice. So, without telling him where we were going we got on a motor bike and rode some three miles to get him a soft drink. I went to the Provincial Senator's residence, as we knew that it was the only place to have a fridge, gas-powered, running on kerosene!

I said, "Excuse me, madam. My friend who has come up from Buenos Aires is very ill. He's got a headache. Could you be so kind as to give me a little bit of ice?"

The truth was that the ice was to make him a cocktail with. We'd just started to drink when all of a sudden the Senator's wife appeared. Ernesto threw himself on the floor and began to pretend that he had a headache. Nevertheless the lady could see that he was faking it. So he just stops pretending and laughs. That's what he was like: just one of the boys, one of us. This is what people want to forget, as later on he rose above this to become an exceptional individual. But if we forget moments like these he becomes a remote figure, aloof; and how then can we live up to the example he has set? In other words, we deify him.

By now it was already six in the evening, he was in a jolly mood and we'd arranged for me to tow him on my motor bike so that he could make up some ground. Then he says to me: "Shorty, I've got to tell you something before I go. You can see that you like leprosy: your work consists of being the local bigwig, screwing anything that moves and throwing as much wine down your neck as you can." So I say to him: "Why don't you just fuck off?" Such recollections show what Che was like, his sense of humor, and what it was like to be his friend.

Another huge example of friendship is the farewell letter that he sent to Fidel when he departed for the Congo in April 1965. Do you really think it was necessary for him to write that his only fault in his relationship with Fidel was "not to have had more faith in you from the start, in the Sierra Maestra; and not to have realized quickly enough your abilities as a leader and revolutionary"?

A man who sailed in a leaky old tub along with 81 men to instigate a Revolution; ready to go with him to the ends of the Earth; and what he wrote was later to be used by opponents of the Revolution as a pretext to attack Fidel! As far as I'm concerned, this is such an obvious expression of friendship.

That's what a true friend is like—telling the truth when the opportunity arises. That's what matters above everything else—you always felt that he made you perform over and above yourself. I'll tell you something else—even now I can't stop asking myself "What would Ernesto say about this?" or "What would Ernesto say about that?" This happens even now, when I have to make an important decision, or even when I have to make a choice over a routine thing.

The thought of a long-distance trip had been bouncing around in my head ever since I was 14 years old. Since then I had read just about everything that had been written and published about just such journeys in the world. I had a work entitled "The Treasures Of Youth," some 20 volumes. I knew them by heart. If I wasn't interested in something I would say "That's for after the journey," whereas if I was interested in something I would take twice the interest in it and would do it before my journey.

Everybody wanted to come with me on the journey. Nevertheless, I met up with the best possible companion, who else but Ernesto Guevara de la Serna? You couldn't hope for better.

So we left, with something to our advantage, the fact that neither of us was scared of leprosy. At that time, little was known about it. Nevertheless, although people were terrified of it, off we'd go knowing that we were determined to treat the poor victims of this disease with kindness and sensitivity. We were convinced that it wasn't contagious, we didn't even take gloves with us; and that opened lots of doors for us. We knew that we would receive a warm welcome. There were times when we disagreed with the doctors as they didn't want us to go into where the patients were without gloves, or eating a water melon; all the same that's what we did. Neither of us showed any revulsion towards leprosy and that was what helped us a lot.

Sometimes I think about those times and I remember Che's sensitivity and kindness, that people have tried to bury, forgetting that he was just another human being like the rest of us; in spite of his unsurpassed abilities as a military tactician, economist, politician, sociologist, philosopher, and artist; not to mention his liking for photography and poetry, subjects he also took an interest in.

He used to turn up to work every morning, ready to do the biopsies. I remember once, on a visit to a leper colony, there was a very attractive, but very sick, girl, with marks all over her body but with a perfect face and hands; and a mark on her arm. Nevertheless, she would always wear a blouse with long sleeves. As soon as she would see a doctor, she would always say "Excuse me, doctor. You know that they don't want me discharged but I'm healthy. And my family want me at home. I live in Tucumán."

Ernesto sticks his oar in and says, "Well, listen to that. Perhaps you go into too much detail. She's in perfect health!"

So I say to him, "I'll show you how the girl really is. Come with me." I start examining her, I get her to take her clothes off, and I give her a gown to put on. I start to examine her using a tub of icy water and another with boiling water, placing these one after another against unaffected areas, whilst the patient says "hot" or "cold" as appropriate. He was looking at me as if to say "I told you so." So I took a hypodermic needle and put it alongside me, without her seeing, as she's got her back to us; and I prick her in an area where I know she can't feel anything. The poor girl says "hot," as she's trying to guess. She couldn't answer at all, as I'd placed the needle against a part that had already been left without feeling due to her illness.

So then Ernesto's face changes, and he says to me, "You bastard! Do you have no shame? Have you lost all your feelings?"

I said, "Ernesto, I just wanted to show you how she really is." That was something that reached into the depths of his heart and touched him, as it did me. Of course, I felt bad about it. I apologised to him, but he kept going on about it…

I also recall the day that we left the lepers of San Pablo. One of the musicians in the orchestra didn't have any fingers, so he had attached some straws to himself so that he could play his instrument. So Ernesto writes his mother a letter for him! In the letter he describes how some of the lepers come up to him whereas others keep their distance. In my opinion, at that moment he was very touched by the kindness of these people. Half a century later, I can see that even then he was moving away from the idea of private medicine and immersing himself in what could be termed the notion of medicine for the people, for the poor. This might appear a little fanciful, maybe so. But that's how I see it.

For a long time afterwards he would continue to keep in touch with some of his ex-patients. One such was a man on whose elbow he had conducted a minor operation. He relished writing to him, as well as to Zoraida Bolearte, the assistant to the director of Lepra in Lima, Peru. He even sent her a postcard from a raft we were sailing in!

He used to seek me out, but as he was a Government Minister I didn't think he should waste his valuable time with me. That's the only thing I regret. I should have gone to see him more.

Every time he went to Santiago de Cuba he would look me up. At that time I was based at the Eastern Medical School there, which I had helped found. Whenever I went to Havana I would call him. I could have just turned up without calling beforehand but I used to say to him, "What time could I see you, if it's not too much bother?" Just by doing that I would be tying him up, and he would say, "Come round at quarter to one and we'll have a few yerba mates."

I was overjoyed to go, but after an hour or so I would say, "I'm off." Yet he would continue to chat for a little longer, but then that was his choice. I'd hold back because I didn't want to take up his time and yes, he knew it. But at the same time I can tell you that I was one of those who could just hop into the lift in the Ministry, even though I had no right to be there.

Before he left for the Congo in April 1965, I think he wanted to say his farewell to me in his own special way, with few words, and perhaps not wishing to be too sentimental, or at least not appearing so. Before he left he gave me the three volumes which make up one of the fundamental accounts of Cuban history, *El Ingenio* (*The Sugar Mill*) by the late Cuban historian Manuel Moreno Fraginals.

The crux of what I'm saying to you can be summed up by what he wrote in there for me—"When the smell of gunpowder eases, I'll be waiting for you, gypsy who wanders no more." And why am I telling you this? Well, some of our arguments were about political power and how to achieve it through revolution. He only believed in armed struggle, whereas I would say that there had to be another way. Of course I respected his arguments, as he did mine. That's also essential in a sincere relationship between two genuine friends. In such cases I remember what Benito Juárez said: "Between people as between countries—respect for the other's rights means peace."

Be in no doubt. In my opinion Che was well aware of this concept and his beliefs, his way of thinking, they all stemmed from the respect he held for himself and others. He showed this all the time, even risking his life to do so, if that was what it took. As a result of his outlook on life, I think the words he wrote for me were a call to join him once the cannons fired off their salute; or in other words, with the arrival of victory, something of which he was always convinced. I remember how he ended his farewell letter to Fidel: "Hasta la Victoria Siempre"—Ever Onward to Victory.

CHE
VIVE

Octubre · LA AMERICA DEL CHE

Homenaje simultáneo de los artistas de Nuestra Améric
Chile (Santiago - Valparaíso)   Instituto de Arte Latinoamericano

Above: **A poster for the Organization for Solidarity among the Peoples of Asia, Africa, and Latin America (OSPAAAL)**

★ Second trip to Latin America

I was linked (to the rebel commander) from the beginning by a bond of liking romantic adventure and the thought that it would be worth dying on a foreign beach for such a pure ideal

As soon as he graduated as a doctor, **Ernesto planned another trip through Latin America**, this time with his good friend Carlos "Calica" Ferrer. They set off on their journey in July 1953, and this time he seems to have been more consciously seeking to develop his **political education**. As he was leaving he called back to his mother as the train pulled away: "Here goes a soldier of the Americas."

Their journey took them to Bolivia, Peru, and Ecuador, where the two friends separated. Calica went on to Caracas to meet up with Alberto Granado, while Ernesto took a boat to Panama, then on through Costa Rica and Honduras to Guatemala.

In Costa Rica **he met six Cubans** who had participated in a failed assault on **26th July 1953** on the **Moncada Barracks** in Santiago de Cuba, the center of President Batista's power in the east of the island. Ernesto was fascinated to learn about this attempt at insurrection, and about its charismatic leader Fidel Castro, who at that time was in a Batista jail on the Isle of Pines (now the Isle of Youth). Batista's government was notorious for its links with the mafia and US business interests, and organized opposition to it had been growing for several years.

When Ernesto reached Guatemala he met up with another Cuban "Moncadista," Ñico López, who first dubbed him

"**Che**," after his Argentine habit of beginning his conversations with "Che," roughly the equivalent of "Hey, you."

Only days after reaching Guatemala in December Che met Hilda Gadea, a Peruvian political activist with the social democratic APRA party. She was three years older than Che, and had more experience of politics. She set about introducing Che to the Russian classics, and the writings of Jean-Paul Sartre and the Chinese revolutionary Mao Tse-tung.

Guatemala was in a state of acute political tension. President Jacobo Arbenz had been elected in March 1951 on a reforming platform, and had set about reducing the economic power of the powerful US United Fruit Company, La Frutera, as it was known throughout Latin America. La Frutera owned 234,000 hectares of land, of which it worked only 15 per cent. It owned ships and railways, employed 10,000 workers, and had strong links with the Morgan and Rockefeller banks. US Secretary of State John Foster Dulles had been one of the lawyers who had made the original contract between United Fruit and the Guatemala state, and his brother Alan was director of the CIA.

Arbenz's expropriation of 84,000 hectares of United Fruit land prompted the CIA to plan his overthrow. On 17th June 1954 they backed an invasion from Honduras, and supported it with an aerial bombardment. **Che threw himself into the resistance to the invasion**, offering to help organize workers' militias, but Arbenz fled to the Mexican Embassy and resigned. Che assisted as a medic and firefighter, but within ten days it was all over and the CIA flew in their new puppet president Carlos Castillo Armas. Nine thousand Guatemalans had been killed or locked up.

Guatemala was a political watershed for Che. He had seen first-hand the savagery with which the United States was prepared to intervene to thwart an attempt at land reform, and it hardened him in his determination to fight for **social justice**.

★ Joining the guerrillas

CHE: What do you think of the Cubans' crazy idea of invading a completely mobilized island?

HILDA: It's crazy alright, but you can't argue with it.

CHE: Just what I think. I wanted to know what you'd say. I've decided to join the expedition.

Hilda Gadea was among those jailed following the overthrow of the Arbenz government in Guatemala, but she quickly obtained her release. She and Che made their ways separately to **Mexico**, where they were reunited in October 1954.

In Mexico Che again met up with the **Cuban Moncadistas**. In June 1955 Ñico López introduced him to **Raúl Castro**, the brother of Fidel, who had also participated in the attack on the Moncada barracks in Santiago de Cuba.

On 8th July, having been released from jail in Cuba, **Fidel Castro** arrived in Mexico City, with plans to prepare an invasion of Cuba. Two days later he and Che met for the first time and talked for ten hours. By the end of the conversation Che had thrown in his lot with the Cubans, and Fidel had accepted him as **a member of the invasion force**.

Che's relationship with Hilda Gadea had grown closer and they decided to marry. The ceremony was on 18th August 1955, in the presence of Raúl Castro and other Cubans. Fidel Castro, suspecting he was under surveillance, arrived later.

During the following months Hilda and Che went visiting Mayan archaeological sites in Chiapas and the Yucatán. Three months later their daughter Hilda Beatriz Guevara was born, on 15th February 1956. By November the couple had separated.

The following month training for the invasion of Cuba got under way in earnest. Che and the Cuban Moncadistas joined a rifle club, and an instructor was found to teach them unarmed combat. Fidel Castro engaged as their military instructor a retired Cuban soldier named Alberto Bayo who had fought with the Spanish foreign legion and then against General Franco in the Spanish Civil War. An isolated **ranch outside Mexico City** was rented as a training barracks.

But the Mexican police were soon on to the trainee soldiers, and on 24th June 30 of them were **arrested** and imprisoned in the **Miguel-Schultz detention center** for foreigners. Fidel Castro was able to secure his release after a week, but Che and one other Cuban were only allowed out after 57 days.

The final stage in preparation for the invasion was to find a boat in which to sail across the Mexican Gulf to the eastern end of Cuba. Eventually a fishing yacht, quaintly named the Granma, was purchased from an American. It was 63 feet long, with seven cabins, but a little cramped for 82 men and all their weapons.

Above: **With two friends, Mexico, 1954**

Ernesto arrived in Mexico at the end of 1954 from Guatemala.

I purchased a camera and together we dedicated ourselves to the clandestine task of taking photographs in the parks, together with a Mexican who had a small laboratory where we developed our photographs. We got to know the whole of Mexico City, walking from one end to the other to deliver our dreadful photographs, fighting with every kind of client to convince them that in truth the little child in the photograph was very beautiful and that it was worth paying one Mexican peso for this wonder.

We burst with heroism but failed to reach the summit. I was ready to die trying and leave my bones behind.

Popocatepetl or "el Popo," as it is known by Mexicans, is situated on the outskirts of Mexico City. During his stay in Mexico, as part of his guerrilla training Che tried to climb it regularly, carrying the Argentine flag in his rucksack.

Above: **With Hilda Gadea, Mexico, 1955**

On 18th August 1955 Che married Hilda Gadea, a Peruvian political activist he had met in Guatemala, in the town of Tepozotlán. A little while later the two visited ruins of the Maya civilization at Palenque, Uxmal, and Chichén Itzá.

Che on becoming a father

Now I'll tell you about the little girl: I'm overjoyed with her, my communist soul has swollen enormously: she looks just like Mao Tse-Tung!

Above: **Ernesto and Hilda Beatriz, Mexico, October 1956**

His first child Hildita was born in Mexico City on 15th February 1956.

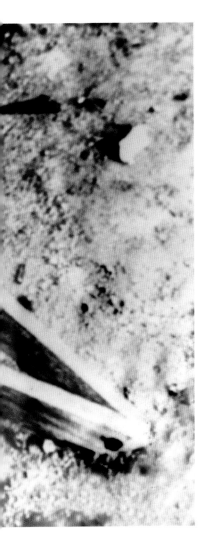

None of Fidel's followers there made a greater effort than Che during our long hikes, exhausting sessions of mountain climbing, personal defense combat practice ... target practice and classes on the theory of guerrilla warfare

Recollection of fellow guerrilla, Jesús Montané Oropesa

Left: **Shooting practice, Mexico City, 1956**

One of the first photos of Che's military training. With other future expeditionaries who were to sail to Cuba on the yacht *Granma*, he practiced shooting at a sports center in Mexico City called Los Gramitos.

Above: **The Miguel-Schultz Immigration Detention Center, Mexico City, 1956**

Many of the Cuban revolutionaries were held under immigration laws after being arrested while training for their invasion of Cuba. In the center of the photo is María Antonia González, a prominent supporter of the future expeditionaries in whose house Che met Fidel Castro at the end of July 1955. Years later, in the farewell letter he wrote to Castro, Che was to refer to this encounter: "I remember the time when I met you in the house of María Antonia, when you proposed to me to come, all the tension of the preparations…" Fidel Castro, in dark glasses, is standing at María Antonia's left side; Che is seated second from left; Juan Almeida is seated in the center, and Ramiro Valdés is on his left.

Che on being arrested

Two Mexican police units, both paid by Batista, were hunting for Fidel Castro, and one of them had the good economic luck to capture him, committing the mistake—also economic—of not killing him, after taking him prisoner. Many of his followers were captured in the next few days; our ranch on the outskirts of Mexico City also fell into the hands of the police and we all went to jail.

A revolution that begins

I got to know him on one of those chilly Mexican nights and I remember that our first argument revolved around international politics. By the small hours that night, by early morning, I had become one of the future expeditionaries.

Right: **Prisoners, Mexico, 1956**

This is the first photograph taken of Fidel Castro and Che together, in the extradition jail. In a letter to his parents from prison on 6th July 1956 Che wrote: "… my future is tied up with the Cuban Revolution. I will either triumph alongside it or die there."

★ To Cuba on the Granma
The asthmatic progress of our launch made the last hours of our voyage interminable

The *Granma* set out from **Tuxpán on the Gulf of Mexico** on 25th November, 1956. Among the **82 men on board** there were only four with experience of sailing and when the sea got rough, as it did for the first three days, the others suffered horribly.

The revolutionaries expected their journey, to Las Coloradas on the south-western tip of eastern Cuba, to take five days, and they had arranged for an uprising in Santiago de Cuba to take place on 30th November to distract the attention of President Batista's armed forces. But the **bad weather at sea** slowed them down, and they didn't reach their destination until 2nd December.

In fact, the *Granma* ran aground in a marshy area, leading Che to comment in his diary that this was **not so much a landing as a shipwreck**. While they were trying to get ashore they were machine gunned from the air, and as soon as they landed eight men went astray.

Within three days the guerrillas were **taken by surprise** at Alegría de Pío, in the mountains of the Sierra Maestra, and came under machine-gun fire. Che seized his weapons and made for cover, but was **grazed by bullets** in the chest and neck. By the end of December only **15 of the original 82 guerrillas remained**, the others being either dead, missing, or taken prisoner. Nevertheless, they scored their first victory on 17th January when they attacked an army garrison at the mouth of the La Plata river.

Fidel Castro had chosen the mountainous area of the **Sierra Maestra** at the eastern end of the island to start the armed struggle against the regime of President Batista because it offered the best conditions for creating a **guerrilla army**. The terrain was wild and covered with tropical vegetation, with mountain peaks reaching to almost 6,000 feet, making it easy for the guerrillas to melt away and hide in the terrain. In fact in early February 1957 Che did exactly that when he went missing for several days.

In the weeks following the landing of the *Granma* the first task was to stay alive and begin recruiting new guerrillas. They were greatly helped in this by a publicity coup in February. Herbert Matthews, a **New York Times** journalist, traveled to the sierra to interview Fidel Castro. The three articles of his that were subsequently published gave a national and **international prestige** to the rebels out of all proportion to their numbers.

Above: **The yacht Granma, on which the 82 revolutionaries sailed from Mexico to eastern Cuba.**

Guerrilla

fighter

Chapter 2

★ Early days in the Sierra Maestra

No sooner had we disembarked, in great haste and carrying only what was essential, than we entered the swamp and were attacked by enemy planes. It had been seven days of continuous hunger and seasickness during the crossing, followed by three more days, terrible ones, on land. Exactly ten days after the departure from Mexico ... after a night march interrupted by fainting, exhaustion, and rest for the troops, we reached a point known paradoxically by the name Alegría ("joy") de Pío.

Most of the **peasants** in the Sierra Maestra lived in primitive conditions, poorly clothed, without medical attention and unable to read and write. The **rebel army**, by contrast, consisted largely of urban, educated young men (and, later, women) with little direct experience of rural conditions—and yet here the rebels were, promising a new Cuba without political repression and social deprivation. They clearly had a lot of convincing to do.

Drawing on his experiences traveling around Latin America and his skills as a doctor, Che's approach was to organize **literacy classes** for peasants in the evenings and provide medical and dental treatment. Many had never seen a doctor before, and Che's fame spread quickly in the sierra.

The rebels were always on the move, often **sleeping under the stars** despite the cold nights high in the mountains. Yet by August 1957 Che was able to establish the first fixed headquarters, at El Hombrito in a high valley. It was equipped with a radio transmitter and even had a bread oven and a rudimentary hospital. El Hombrito was destroyed in December, but within a few days Che established a new headquarters at La Mesa, to the east of the Turquino, the highest peak in Cuba. Following Che's example, in May 1958 Castro established a headquarters at La Plata, on the west side of the Turquino.

Propaganda was a priority for the rebels, to combat the Batista regime's efforts to minimize their importance. In December 1957 the first edition of the newspaper **El Cubano Libre** (*The Free Cuban*) appeared, with Che acting as its political editor. In his first article he justified the destruction of a sugar mill by the rebels, even though this affected the livelihoods of workers.

In February 1958 Che established the radio station **Radio Rebelde** (Rebel Radio) on the peak Altos de Conrado, with transmitters powerful enough to be heard in Miami and Caracas. In May this was transferred to Castro's headquarters at La Plata.

The same month Che opened a military school in Minas del Frío.

Strict **military discipline** was imposed by Che and the other leaders. Deserters and *chivatos* (informers) faced a military tribunal and, if found guilty, were punished by death.

Until May 1958 the section of the **26th July Movement** which operated in the **llano (the plains)** and which provided the armaments and many of the new recruits for the guerrilla struggle retained some autonomy with respect to the section under Fidel Castro's leadership in the Sierra. Castro gave his support to the general strike called by the *llano* leadership for 9th April 1958, but when it failed Castro moved to take full control of the movement from the Sierra. The following month he called a meeting of the two sections at Mompié in the Sierra Maestra. He invited Che to this meeting even though he was not at that time a member of the revolutionary leadership. As an intellectual with a good knowledge of Marxism, but with no previous political affiliation, Che played a crucial role in bringing together those from the Ortodóxo Party with those from the Cuban Communist Party. In June 1957, still with only **200 armed men**, he called for "all rifles, bullets, resources for the Sierra." Fidel Castro's success was such that by the end of the first year of fighting, moderate opponents of Batista and leaders of the Cuban Communist Party were coming from Havana to talk to him.

Right: **HERIBERTO ECHEVARRÍA**, Havana, 1980

Following page: **Peasants and rebels, Sierra Maestra, 1957**
Fidel Castro and his guerrilla column in conversation with peasants, who were joining the struggle in growing numbers and helping to create a secure base for military operations.

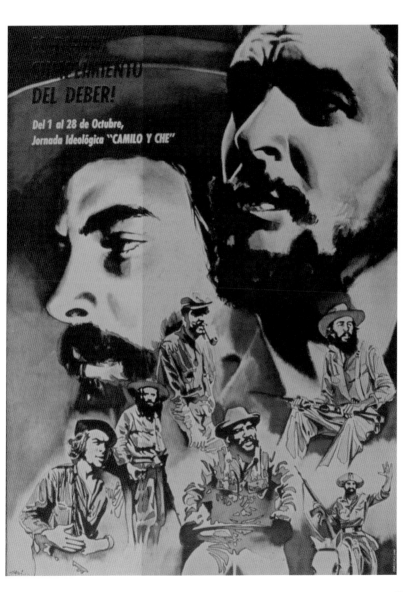

CUMPLIMIENTO DEL DEBER!

Del 1 al 28 de Octubre,
Jornada Ideológica "CAMILO Y CHE"

I was confronted with the dilemma of dedicating myself to medicine or my duty as a revolutionary soldier. I had in front of me a rucksack full of medicine and an ammunition case, the two weighed too much to carry together. I took the ammunition and left the rucksack behind.

Left: **The doctor soldier, Sierra Maestra, 1957**

Che took up smoking cigars when he reached Cuba, claiming it helped his asthma and repelled mosquitoes. He joined the rebels as a doctor, but quickly displayed the qualities needed by a guerrilla fighter.

Che on the role of the guerrilla doctor

The doctor achieves to the full his role of a true priest who seems to carry for the men, in his poorly equipped knapsack, the necessary consolation. It is beyond calculation what a simple aspirin means for someone who is suffering, administered by the friendly hand of one who feels and makes their sufferings his own.

Above: **Doctor in the Sierra Maestra, April 1957**
In the early days of the guerrilla campaign Che had
responsibilities as both a doctor and a soldier. Here he is tending
the hand of a fighter wounded in an accident, with Camilo
Cienfuegos helping. Behind are Haydée Santamaría and Fidel
Castro. The image is taken from a movie film made in the Sierra
Maestra by the US journalist Robert Taber and cameraman
Wendell Hoffman.

Fidel calculated that the army was on the way to ambush us and that sooner or later it would find us; so he decided to prepare an ambush for the enemy soldiers in this region

Left: **Preparing an attack, Sierra Maestra, 1957**
One of the best known photos of the Sierra Maestra campaign. Fidel Castro is drawing in the earth to explain tactics. From left to right, Che, Juan Almeida, Ramiro Valdés, and Calixto García.

One of the heroes of our struggle, Comandante Crescencio Pérez, entered the Sierra at 65 years of age and was immediately one of the most useful men in the troop

Left: **Captains, Sierra Maestra, May 1957**

Fidel Castro with Crescencio Pérez, a peasant whose knowledge of the mountains was invaluable to the guerrillas. Also in the group are Guillermo García, Che, Universo Sánchez, Raúl Castro, Jorge Sotus and Juan Almeida. The photo was taken by the North American journalist Andrew Saint George.

Above: **Minas del Frío, Sierra Maestra, 1958**

In April 1958 Che moved into the zone of operations of Column 1 in Minas del Frío to take charge of the school for rebel recruits organized by Fidel Castro. He took responsibility for the defense of the western zone as the principal support for Castro in the offensive against Batista's army. The battle lasted for 72 days, and resulted in victory for the rebels.

We walked until night made it impossible to go further and we decided to sleep all together, huddled up, attacked by mosquitoes, racked by thirst and hunger

Left: **Fighters, Sierra Maestra, 17th February 1957**

The first meeting of the leadership of the 26th July Movement after the beginning of the Sierra Maestra campaign was at the farm of Epifanio Díaz. On that day various photographs were taken, mostly by Frank País who was the leader of the struggle in the *llano* (the urban struggle.) He is on the right. This is the first photograph of Che as a guerrilla fighter. Also in the photograph are Universo Sánchez and Manuel Fajardo.

Above: **The initiation, Sierra Maestra, 1958**

The guerrillas played baseball (Cuba's national sport) in their moments of free time in the Sierra Maestra, and tried to teach it to Che, whose main athletic pastimes back home in Argentina were soccer and rugby.

After the disaster of the engagement of Alegría de Pío, reduced to some 15 men and physically and even morally done in, we reunited and were only able to go forward because of the enormous confidence that Fidel Castro displayed in those decisive moments, because of his example as a revolutionary leader and his inexhaustible faith in the people

Right: **La Mesa camp, Sierra Maestra, 1958**
Fidel Castro (left) and Che (right) discussing tactics during a moment of relaxation.

I quickly felt the disagreeable sensation, a little like burning or numbed flesh, announcing the entry of a bullet into my unprotected left foot

Right: **After the battle, Sierra Maestra, 1957**

At the end of 1957 Che was injured while fighting in Altos de Conrado, one of the guerrilla incursions of the Column 4 which he commanded. His convalescence gave him the chance to indulge his passion for reading, including Emil Ludwig's biography of the German poet Goethe, in the company of a pet dog he had acquired.

Above: **Column 4, Sierra Maestra, July 1957**
Column 4, led by Che, was the first troop formed from the original guerrilla force. It began its operations at the end of July 1957 in the eastern zone of the Turquino mountain peak. The photo was taken at El Hombrito, the first permanent guerrilla base to be established.

Letter to his parents

Dear folks

I'm fine. I've just spent two and have five left (speaking of cat's lives). I'm still working in the same line. News is patchy and will continue to be, but take my word that God is an Argentinian.

Tete

Che on pride

There's a bit of vanity hiding somewhere within all of us. It made me feel like the proudest man in the world that day.

Che had joined the Cuban rebels as their doctor, but within a few weeks of reaching Cuba he proved to have exceptional **capabilities as a soldier**. This was ironic in view of the fact that he had been rejected for military service as a student in Argentina on account of his asthma.

He soon demonstrated an extraordinary disregard for danger and an **ability to inspire and lead**, combined with a shrewd sense of tactics. These qualities were quickly recognized by Fidel Castro, who on 22nd July 1957 **appointed him commander**, the highest rank in the rebel army and equivalent to major. Castro at that time was the only other guerrilla to have that rank.

The promotion was made quite casually. Castro was dictating a letter to his brother Raúl offering condolences to Frank País, the 26th July Movement leader in Santiago de Cuba, for the death of his brother at the hands of Batista's police. When Raúl asked what rank he should put after Che's name, Castro told him to put "*comandante*."

Castro's aide, Celia Sánchez, presented Che with a **five-pointed star** representing the national insignia of the Cuban flag. Later, he was to wear the star proudly on his beret.

Right: **A poster for the Organization for Solidarity among the Peoples of Asia, Africa, and Latin America (OSPAAAL)**

Che on Fidel

It is a political experience to have met Fidel, the revolutionary Cuban. He is a young man who is intelligent, very sure of himself and extremely audacious: I believe that we have a lot in common.

Above: **Secrets, Sierra Maestra, 1957**

Fidel Castro and Che.

Right: **Montería, Sierra Maestra, February 1958**

Che and Fidel Castro in conversation with Evelio Laferte, first director of the school belonging to the Rebel Army in the Sierra Maestra. Laferte was the first enemy army officer to join the ranks of the guerrillas.

★ From the Escambray to victory in Havana

The army with its spinal column snapped ... was not yet beaten and had to continue the struggle

After a year and a half of fighting and organizing, the **rebel army was gaining the upper hand** and going onto the offensive. On 21st June 1958 it won a decisive victory at El Jigüey, after 11 days of fighting against a much larger force.

On 21st August Fidel ordered Che to lead his Column 8, with 142 men, to **Las Villas province** in the center of the island. **Camilo Cienfuegos** was to lead his Column 2, of 82 men, to Pinar del Río province in the west of the island. They left the Sierra on 31st August, Che expecting to reach his destination in four days.

The trucks they had been planning to travel in were destroyed, and the journey took Che's column 47 days on foot and with horses. They had to contend with three **hurricanes** which cut the roads they had been planning to use. Che reached the **Escambray mountains** on 16th October. He established a base at **El Pedrero** and opened a military school. The plan was to cut the country in two by taking the regional capital of Santa Clara.

In the event Che was able to proceed towards his goal surprisingly fast. He won important battles at **Fomento** on 18th December and **Placetas** on 23rd December. Four days later he was at **Santa Clara** and preparing to sabotage an armored train filled with soldiers and armaments, which was on its way from Havana. On 29th December the rebels derailed the train, causing it to explode. By 1st January 1959 Santa Clara was taken, and two days later Che was in **Havana**.

We walked through difficult terrain, suffering attacks by swarms of mosquitoes that made the rest periods unbearable, eating little and poorly, drinking water from swampy rivers or simply from swamps. Each day of travel became longer and truly horrible. We were hungry, thirsty, and could hardly advance because our legs were as heavy as lead and the weapons were enormously heavy. We continued advancing...

Only a far off sight brought his face to life and imbued the guerrilla with new courage. That sight ... was a blue band towards the west, the blue band of the mountains of Las Villas.

Left: **Riding in the Escambray mountains, Las Villas, 1958**

During the Las Villas campaign, Che rode on horseback through the Escambray Mountains. The photo was taken at Caballete de Casa.

Against brute force and injustice the People will have the last word, that of Victory

Left: **Fomento, Las Villas, 1958**

At the beginning of November 1958 the final offensive was prepared. On Fidel Castro's orders, Che was put in command of the Ciro Redondo Column Number 8, with its primary objective to advance into Central Cuba. With scarcely any time to recuperate, they flushed the enemy out of various inhabited areas, amongst them Fomento, the first municipal area in Las Villas province captured by Che en route to achieving the surrender of the whole region.

Here we are. The word comes to us damp from the Cuban forests. We have climbed the Sierra Maestra and we have known the dawn; and our minds and hands are full of the seed of dawn. And we are ready to sow it on this land and defend it so that it may bear fruit.

Left: **Broadcasting, Escambray, Las Villas, 1958**

Che was the founder of the radio station Radio Rebelde, which began broadcasting in February 1958 from the Sierra Maestra. Its role was to bring new ideas to the Cuban people and inform them of the victories of the Rebel Army. With the transfer of his command to Caballete de Casa, in Las Villas province, he continued to run the radio station from there.

People—forward with the Revolution! Workers to the struggle! Peasants—organize! The Revolutionary Army goes on with its already unstoppable and victorious offensive and soon the whole of Las Villas Province will be declared Free Cuban Territory.

Right: **El Pedrero, Las Villas, 23rd December 1958**

After the victory in Cabaiguán, a village located in the center of Cuba, Che held one of his many meetings with his troops.

We had a bazooka without shells and we had to fight against a dozen tanks, but we also knew that, to do so effectively, we had to reach the residential areas of the city, where tanks are much less useful

Right: **Placetas, Las Villas, December 1958**

As the war neared its conclusion Che worked on his plans for the capture of Santa Clara, the most decisive battle of the Las Villas campaign, from his room in the Las Tullerías Hotel. Che wanted to be sure that his column would not be exposed to aerial attacks or enemy tanks.

Che on women fighters

In the tough life of the fighter, a woman is a comrade who brings the qualities peculiar to her sex but with the ability to work just as hard as a man. She can fight, she is weaker but no less resistant than he is.

Left: **Remedios, Las Villas, December 1958**

Che in the company of his future wife Aleida March at the entrance to the recently captured barracks of Batista's army in the town of Remedios. Days before, during the capture of Cabaiguán, Che had fractured his left wrist climbing a wall. Aleida March is offering him a bar of soap.

We had been able to take the power station and the city's whole north-west side, broadcasting the news that Santa Clara was in the hands of the Revolution

Right: **Victory at hand, Santa Clara, Las Villas, 1958**

The people of Santa Clara welcome the rebels. Che is accompanied by Aleida March.

It is the finale and it is unfolding
With an unmatchable din.
One hundred thousand thunderclaps crash,
And their song is profound.
In the mouth of the finale,
You can hear valor fly.

Poem by Che

Left: **The Battle of Santa Clara, Las Villas, 1958**

Santa Clara, capital of Las Villas Province and strategically located, was the site of one of Fulgencio Batista's strongest fortresses. Che's mission was to unite all of the opposition forces and to prevent the arrival of government reinforcements from the eastern region. The capture of the city marked the collapse of Batista's will to fight.

This wonderful victory of the People over its oppressors has to be strengthened with the help of all...

Left: **The surrender, Fomento, Las Villas, 1958**

A soldier from Batista's army surrenders to join the Rebel Army, and is welcomed by Che.

I can't say I'm Che's secretary, because I'm a fighter. I fought beside him in the Las Villas campaign and took part in all the engagements there. That makes me his orderly... When it became practically impossible for me to continue living in Santa Clara, due to my revolutionary activities, I decided to join the ranks of those fighting the dictatorship by taking up arms.

Recollection of Aleida March, Che's partner

Right: **The Cabaña fortress, Havana, January 1959**

On Fidel Castro's orders, Che advanced with his column to the city of Havana, occupying the Cabaña fortress, the capital's second most important military installation, in the early hours of 3rd January 1959. The presence of the legendary guerrilla immediately sparked the interest of the press and he gave interviews to international newspapers and magazines.

Down from the eastern hills where he had forged his big victory, Fidel Castro last week marched in tumultuous triumph through the towns and villages of post-Batista Cuba. He came not as a dutifully honored conqueror but as a man ecstatically acclaimed by the people he had liberated... They screamed *"Viva!,"* thundered applause, and flung torrents of flowers when Castro and his *barbudos* (bearded ones) appeared.

Life magazine, 19th January 1959

Left: **Fidel Castro's entry into Havana, 8th January 1959**

On 3rd January, three days after President Batista fled the island, Fidel Castro set out on a leisurely triumphal parade by road from the east of the island, reaching Havana after five days. The city was electrified.

Let's go,
Ardent prophet of the dawn,
Along recondite
unmarked tracks,
To liberate the green cayman
you love so much.

Poem by Che for Fidel Castro

Right: **Meeting in the Cabaña fortress, Havana, 1959**

After making his first speech in the capital, Fidel
Castro had a meeting with Che in the Cabaña fortress.
The "green cayman" Che refers to in his poem is a
reference to the island of Cuba which is often
popularly referred to in this way because of its shape.

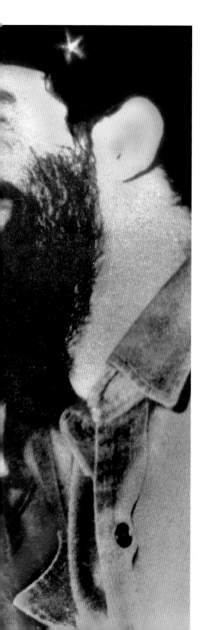

More than my comrade in battle, of joys and victories, Camilo was truly a brother

Left: **Friends, Sancti Spiritus, Las Villas, 3rd May 1959**

Che with another comandante, Camilo Cienfuegos, who was to disappear in October 1959 when the plane he was traveling in went missing over the sea. Che and Camilo were diametrically opposed characters, formed by different cultural upbringings. Nevertheless, they were united by a close friendship from the early days of the guerrilla campaign in the Sierra Maestra. Years later Che would dedicate his book *Guerrilla Warfare* to his close friend, and give his first son the name of Camilo.

Che on Camilo

Few men have succeeded in leaving on every action such a distinctive personal mark ... he had the natural intelligence of the people who had chosen him out of thousands for a privileged position on account of the audacity of his blows, his tenacity, his intelligence, and unequalled devotion. Camilo practiced loyalty like a religion.

Right: **Raúl Martinez, 1982**

He rushed into her arms and couldn't hold back the tears

Recollection of Ernesto Guevara senior

Left: **The embrace, Havana Airport, 9th January 1959**

Che's reunion with his mother after a long separation was later described by his father Ernesto Guevara: "A crowd of photographers and TV cameras were there to record the moment. A little later I would embrace my son. We hadn't seen each other for six years."

Below: **Mother and son, Havana, 9th January, 1959**

Shortly after the success of the Revolution, Che's family traveled to Cuba from Argentina.

Commander, what was the most emotional moment during your life as a guerrilla?

When I heard my father's voice on the telephone, speaking from Buenos Aires. I hadn't been back to my country in six years.

Above: **Afternoon snooze, Havana, 1959**

Che has fallen asleep beside his mother Celia after lunch at a friend's house. His brother Juan Martín is on his left. Six years later, when he was fighting in the Congo, he learnt of his mother's death in Buenos Aires. In a meditation on loss he wrote:

I only know that I have a physical need for my mother to appear and for me to rest my head on her thin lap, and for her to say to me "mi viejo," with simple, full tenderness and to feel on my skin her unsteady hand

Left: **Reunion, Havana Airport, 9th January 1959**

Che with his parents Celia and Ernesto.

Statesman, ambass

or, husband, father

Chapter 3

★ Creating a new Cuba
We love life and we will defend it

The **entry into Havana** of the guerrillas at the beginning of January 1959 was the beginning, not the end, of the story. Beyond the immediate tasks of establishing a **new government** and ensuring the **security** of the country lay the fundamental issue of satisfying the social and economic aspirations that the struggle against Batista had awakened.

Fidel Castro played out his hand of the reforming nationalist leader who was going to clean up the corruption of the old regime, taking care not to arouse the suspicions and hostility of the US government. He made a first trip to the US in April 1959, during which he met with **Vice President Richard Nixon**.

Che, like Castro, had always been convinced that the North Americans would eventually be hostile to the Revolution. They had, after all, armed and supported Batista until the last months of the war, and he had witnessed first hand how they had crushed the government of Jacobo Arbenz in Guatemala in 1954. In the Sierra the guerrillas had already **redistributed land** to peasant families, and Che was eager to push on with their embryonic social program. In the first months of the Revolution he met constantly with a group of advisers to develop plans.

In June Che was sent abroad as Cuba's **ambassador at large** to establish relations with other countries of the "non-aligned" Third World. He was away for three months, and visited 12 countries. He met President Nasser in Egypt, Prime Minister Nehru in India, President Tito in Yugoslavia, and President Sukarno in Indonesia. He also visited Japan where he was impressed at how a nation without oil or other strategic raw materials was able to industrialize rapidly following agrarian reform.

On his return Che was put **in charge of industrialization** within the National Institute of Agrarian Reform, then in November he was made **President of the Central Bank**, with a remit of overseeing plans for the economic development of the country. The following month he signed the **agrarian reform law** which expropriated farms of more than 400 hectares. This meant nationalizing the holdings of US monopolies such as United Fruit, with four per cent bonds over 20 years as compensation.

At this time the **Soviet Union** was making its first offers of credits and industrial cooperation in exchange for Cuban sugar.

A year later, in January 1961, a **Ministry of Industry** was created, with Che its minister. The wave of nationalizations of foreign firms had created a need for central management, as had the opening up of trade relations with the Soviet Union, which offered the possibility of developing heavy industry for the first time in Cuba.

Relations with the United States steadily soured during these years, as Washington saw the interests of US monopolies challenged. On 3rd January 1961 **President Eisenhower** broke diplomatic relations with Havana, as a prelude to a period of more open hostility towards the troubled island.

There is absolutely no need to marvel that a foreigner should come to fight for Cuba ... I confess that I have never felt a foreigner, neither in Cuba nor in any of the other countries I have visited. I have had rather an adventurous life. I have felt Guatemalan in Guatemala, Mexican in Mexico, Peruvian in Peru, as today I feel Cuban in Cuba and naturally as I feel Argentinian in Argentina. Here and everywhere, that is the basis of my personality, I cannot forget yerba mate and roast meat.

Left: CARMELO GONZÁLEZ, "Che's America," 1973, Casa de las Américas collection

Che on power

How easy it is to govern when one follows a system of consulting the will of the people and one holds as the only norm all the actions which contribute to the well being of the people

Right: **Cuban women, Havana, 1959**

In the early months of 1959 Che is accompanied by his future wife, Aleida March and Fidel Castro's mother Lina Ruz (right). They are sending off a delegation invited to a women's congress in Chile.

There is no effort made towards the people that is not repaid with the people's trust

Left: **The welcome, Havana Airport, May 1959**

Che and a group of fellow revolutionaries at José Martí airport in Havana await Fidel Castro's return from a tour of South American countries.

The people's heroes cannot be separated from the people, cannot be elevated onto a pedestal, into something alien to the lives of that people...

154

Che on truth

The only passion which guides me is for the truth ... I look at everything from this point of view

Left: **May Day, Santiago de Cuba, 1959**

Four months after the Revolution achieved power Che took part in the May Day festivities held in Santiago de Cuba.

Right: **Wedding in the Cabaña Fortress, Havana, 2nd June 1959**

Che and Aleida March married on 2nd June, in the house of Che's bodyguard, Alberto Castellanos, in the Cabaña Fortress, where Che had his command. Among the guests were Raúl Castro, Vilma Espín, Harry Villegas, and Alberto Castellanos.

Following page: **The wedding car, Havana, 2nd June 1959**

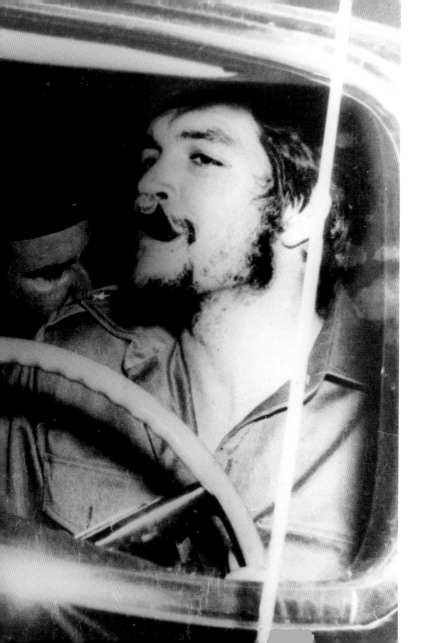

Above: **Guerrilla wedding, Havana, 1959**

Celia Sánchez was the first woman to join the struggle in the Sierra Maestra, in the earliest days of the guerrilla campaign. Due to her knowledge of the region she was the chief organizer of the peasants who supported the guerrillas. A sensitive and resolute woman, she was deeply loved and respected. When Fidel Castro decided to appoint Che as a commander, he gave Celia the task of presenting him with his commander's star, on 21st July 1957.

We heard all sorts of contradictory news: Celia Sánchez has been arrested; Celia Sánchez has been killed, etc... We did not know what to believe, and some of the reports were really frightening, since Celia, for example, was our only safe, confidential contact. Her arrest would mean isolation for the rest of us. Fortunately, the news about Celia turned out to be false.

Interview with
Colonel Alberto Castellanos

Above: **Colonel Alberto Castellanos**

Born in the Sierra Maestra. He was a member of Che's Column 8 which cut the island in two with its victory in the battle of Santa Clara. After the Revolution he was Che's personal bodyguard. He participated with Jorge Ricardo Masetti in the guerrilla campaign in Argentina in 1963. He is currently a retired colonel of the Revolutionary Armed Forces.

Interview in Havana, 13th January 2003

Che was always an object lesson, teaching by example. He had an interesting set of values with which to weigh up people: courageous, hard-working, honest, and honorable. In my case, for example, I was a rebellious type. We would argue frequently during our time in the Sierra Maestra, then later on during the invasion of Santa Clara and afterwards in Havana. Nevertheless, we became friends. I was to be his personal aide and formed part of his entourage.

Che didn't want those among his entourage to have motor cars. We would always be lent cars, at that time from the second-in-command of La Cabaña fortress. They would lend us their cars, but as usually happens, some blabbermouths turned up and told Che what was going on. One day he got together everyone who had been lending us their cars to get them not to do it anymore. Given that this was an order, what were we to do? Well, we stole the cars!

At that time we were simple peasants who didn't know Havana. We would wait until Che put the lights out, in other words went to sleep in his quarters in La Cabaña. Then we would push the cars along, start them up and go off to get to know Havana. Imagine the group—Harry Villegas, Argudín, Hermes Peña—who was to die in Argentina together with Massetti. We desperately wanted to get to know the capital: that's what I mean by our rebelliousness and lack of discipline. For example, both Hermes and Argudín were illiterate; and Harry and myself had only reached seventh grade. Later, Che was to teach them both to read and write, as well as sending us to continue with our studies.

The four of us formed his personal entourage, although this came about by accident, by fate. I started to be by his side after he broke his arm during the assault on Cabaiguan, in December 1958. At that time I had just arrived in the Command and Che needed a driver. So I voluntarily offered my services.

At that time the final offensive was unfolding with attacks on Placetas, Remedios, Caibarién, and elsewhere, followed by the launch of the assault on the most significant strategic location in the center of the country, Santa Clara. When we entered Santa Clara he assigned squads to my command, to Hermes', to Argudín's; and he made Harry Villegas head of the detachment. This little troop of the four of us would later become the Command Garrison. After defeating the regular army and capturing Santa Clara we went onwards to Havana.

On entering Havana, given that I was the only one capable of commanding my squad, I had to instruct the rest. I couldn't return home to Victoria de las Tunas, in Oriente province. My mother thought that I had been killed. She came to see me, but there was no room anywhere and they didn't have anywhere to stay. So I was advised to talk to Che. I said to him:

"Listen, Che. I've got a problem. I've got my mother, my girlfriend, and a niece of mine who have all come to see me as they thought I was dead."

Che said, "And what's the problem?"

"Well, every boarding house is full and Núñez told me to bring them to your house. But where are they going to eat?"

And he replied: "Here with me. Just the same as you and Núñez."

As you can see, it was through such things that we would learn from Che every day. They were generous gestures and as a result friendship was to grow between the boss and his subordinates. One day we were coming back from Santa Clara when he said to me:

"Do you think I could get married in your house?"

I replied: "How can you not think that you can get married in my house, if you gave it to me?"

"Good! I'll get married in your house."

I was overjoyed to be given the chance to share this moment with them, as I had witnessed how their love for each other had grown since the Escambray. I remember that Aleida had come up to the mountains as her underground activities in Santa Clara had led to her persecution by the dictatorship. She arrived at the time the enemy was mounting an offensive against us and she had no choice but to stay. Aleida was very pretty. I thought that she was an extremely attractive young woman, as any man would. With time I realized that they had a lot in common.

Their love for each other was born in the midst of war. She would accompany us everywhere: Cabaiguán, Placetas, Caibarién, Remedios. Che was a very good looking man. He was to devote himself to the Revolution, Aleida, and the children.

When we got to La Cabaña, he gave her a room with a bathroom that was linked between her room and his own. We knew what was going on between them, but they were very discreet. He took care of her. I'm speaking from the heart when I say that it was special, a beautiful relationship; and I believe that she also talks about Che's sensitivity, that she considers him to be straightforward and a man of the people, in addition to his exceptional qualities.

Before marriage was being discussed, we visited the beach house in Tarará where we were going to stay. Whilst I was examining the contents of a cupboard I found two cases of cider. I said to Aleida:

"Shit! Look what I've found! I'll put one aside for your wedding day and the other's for me as I'll be getting married soon."

That day there was a cake being prepared in the La Cabaña pastry shop, along with the case of cider. Camilo Cienfuegos arrived and he asked me what we had for the wedding. I told him the tale of the case of cider and that only Aleida knew about it, as were Che to find out he would have had me punished. So then, of course, straight away Camilo took charge of organizing the wedding. He dispatched all the commanders to bring rum, beer, whatever was required.

The wedding took place after dark and Fidel, Raúl, Vilma, Harry, Celia, and loads of other comrades turned up. I was outside having a drink when all of a sudden I was called by Camilo. Fidel and Raúl were about to sign as witnesses to the wedding; and Che had asked that I be found too, so that I could be his witness. The wedding was on 2nd June 1959, 12 days before Che's 31st birthday. He was happy.

Left: **First journey, Havana, 13th June 1959**

In June 1959 Che left Cuba for three months to visit various countries of the Third World, with the brief of establishing preliminary contacts. These destinations included Egypt, India, Indonesia, Yugoslavia, and Ceylon, and he also visited Japan. This photo of Che with Fidel Castro was taken just before his departure.

Above: **First foreign trip, Havana airport, 13th June 1959**

On 13th June, just 11 days after his marriage, Che left Cuba for a three-month trip visiting countries of the Third World. He was seen off at the airport by Aleida and other comrades.

Letter to his mother

The sense of the masses as opposed to the personal has greatly developed in me. I am always the same solitary person that I was, searching for my way without personal help, but I now have a sense of my historical duty ... I am content that I feel I am someone in life ... I don't know why I'm writing you this, maybe it's merely longing for Aleida. Take it as it is a letter written one stormy night in the skies of India, far from my fatherland and loved ones.

Nehru welcomed us with the amiable familiarity of a patriarchal grandfather but with a noble interest in the anxieties and struggles of the Cuban people, giving us extraordinarily valuable advice and giving us a display of his unconditional sympathy for our cause

Above: **India, 1st July 1959**

Che visited India during his tour of the Third World countries which were members of the Bandung Pact, and met with Prime Minister Jawaharlal Nehru.

Our accord with the Eastern Bloc is partly through urgency; and partly through choice

Above: **Yugoslavia, August 1959**

During his first trip abroad as representative of the new Cuban government, Che arrived in Yugoslavia on 17th August where he was received by President Josip Broz Tito. Omar Fernández, Cuba's Minister of Labor who accompanied Che, also appears in the photo.

Above: **Bayamo, Oriente, 1959**

Che and Aleida at a meal in Bayamo in the house of an old comrade.

Above: **Santiago de Cuba, Oriente, 17th October 1959**

In September 1959 Che was put in charge of industrialization within the newly-created National Institute for Agrarian Reform. On 17th October he took part in the Sugar Assembly held by workers in Oriente province.

We do not put any preconditions whatsoever upon the United States ... we do not put any preconditions whatsoever upon establishing relations; but at the same time we are not prepared to accept any preconditions ourselves...

...the United States government wants us to
pay a high price for this non-peaceful co-existence
that we currently enjoy; and the price that we are
in a position to pay only buys us something
approaching dignity. It goes no further.

We are a lit torch, ... we are that same mirror that we are as individuals for the Cuban people; and we are that mirror so that the peoples of all the Americas may look upon themselves

Above: **Crowd outside the former Presidential Palace, Havana, 26th October 1959**

On 26th October 1959 the leadership of the Revolution summoned a huge demonstration in front of what had been the Presidential Palace, to reject counter-revolutionary provocation emanating from the US.

Left and Above: **The State Bank, Havana, 1959**

Che was made Chairman of the State Bank on 27th November 1959. He spent long hours in his office, reading, writing speeches, and studying mathematics as he guided the government's developing economic policy.

Che on the National Bank

When I became President of the Bank ... we saw that it was not just a case of wanting or not wanting to do things which stalled the banking institutions ... it was the way the system itself was set up. Even when in those conditions the representatives of foreign banks did not use different criteria from us, they were nevertheless spies who could control the whole Bank. Moreover they participated in various credit committees, and all the functions, guidelines, and foundations of the new policy were laid bare, in some situations, in really delicate matters, and were inspected by their representatives. Furthermore, credits were granted in an anarchic way, and the banks which had the capacity to create money did so by directing credit in the way that was most profitable, ignoring completely the nation's interests.

Above: Che's image has been used on bank notes and stamps since his death. While President of the National Bank it was his duty to sign the new 10 and 20 peso bank notes, which he did by simply writing "Che."

Che on leadership

The man who leads motivates others to catch up with him; encourages those behind up to his level much more than he who pushes from behind with just a word

Above: **Anniversary in Santa Clara, Las Villas, 1959**

In December 1959 Che revisited Santa Clara to celebrate the first
anniversary of one of the most decisive battles of the guerrilla
war, which he had led.

I work 16 to 18 hours a day, sleep for six hours a day whenever I can, and more often than not for less

Above: **Havana, 1960**

Che took to smoking cigars from his earliest days in the Sierra Maestra, but rarely smoked cigarettes.

Right: **The surprise, Havana, 1959**

Che, like many of the other leaders of the Revolution, worked incredibly long hours and had to grab meals when he could.

This Revolution has always relied on the willingness of the Cuban people

Right: **May Day, Santiago de Cuba, 1960**

For the first two years of the Revolution Che returned to Santiago de Cuba, the capital of the eastern province of Oriente, to take part in the May Day celebrations.

I retain a deep-seated Argentinian aspect due to my upbringing, yet at the same time I feel as much a Cuban as anyone else...

Left: **Reflecting in his office, Havana, 1960**

Che's office was also his refuge, where he would spend long days working intensely. There he would meet influential figures such as Jean-Paul Sartre and Simone de Beauvoir.

★ The Revolution's first film
Tales of the Revolution

Tales of the Revolution was the first production made by the Cuban Film Institute (ICAIC) and the first feature film directed by Tomás Gutiérrez Alea ("Titón"), who went on to become Cuba's greatest film director. It was a challenge to make with scarce resources. It has three parts: *The Wounded*, *Rebels*, and *Santa Clara*.

The second part, *Rebels*, is based on a history of Che Guevara put together from information supplied by many people, and the actors were not, for the most part, professionals but actual rebels. It was filmed in the Sierra Maestra where the original action had taken place.

In an interview Titón spoke about Che's role in the making of the film:

"It was logical that he should dedicate some of his time to us given the importance that the leaders of this country gave to the cinema. What happened in Cuba was not a traditional change of government, as generally occurs in Latin America even today. Here a radical change was taking place and it was important to rescue the memory of the events directly from their protagonists. Thus we spent a whole night with Che, who recounted one anecdote after another. The majority of the stories that he told, and which reveal his personality, had a similar tone: in none of them did he appear as the hero. The hero would usually be some one whom Che had considered to be a coward. Events had made him realize that he had been mistaken in his assessment and he felt the need to express this. There was also in this meeting an assistant of Che, who later became Minister of Finance, Francisco García Vals, who recounted the anecdote which we used in the film..."

While the episode was being filmed, Che suddenly turned up in the Sierra Maestra:

"Up to that moment Che did not know that this story about him was being filmed. Neither did he know that any filming was going on in that place. His visit was by chance: his mother, who had come from Buenos Aires, was in Cuba, and he took her to the Sierra so that she would know the places where he had fought. But the coincidence goes further still: the following day we were to film an ambush, and when Che learnt this he told us that he had made one in this same place. He gave us military advice and really it was he who was responsible for that part of the script with his experience."

From an interview with Silvia Oroz in Havana, 1985

Above and following six pages: On the set of *Tales of the Revolution,* the Sierra Maestra, 1960

Che's personality and appearance made quite an impression among the girls at the ministry, and some were even in love with him. He was a man whom nature had given handsome features. He was very masculine, with beautiful eyes. He spoke with those eyes.

Recollection of Industry Ministry employee, Veronica Fernández

Right: **Havana, 1960**

It is notable that, even in the second year of the Revolution, large images of Che were being prepared, as here where workers of the Graphic Arts Enterprise had prepared an enormous portrait with which to greet him.

It's nothing special, but at least it's something and I think you can always be proud of your father, just as he is of you

Above and Right: **Hildita's Birthday, Havana, 15th February 1960**

Che's first child, Hildita, was born in 1956 while he was living in Mexico City, preparing with Fidel Castro and the other Cuban revolutionaries for their invasion of the island. In the top photograph Che is together with his Peruvian first wife, Hilda Gadea, who had come to live in Cuba after the Revolution.

If you can tremble with indignation every time an injustice is committed in the world, we are comrades

Left: **March to commemorate the victims of La Coubre, Havana, 5th March 1960**

This march was held to commemorate those who died when the French freighter *La Coubre* exploded in Havana harbor. It is led, from left to right; by Prime Minister Fidel Castro, President Osvaldo Dorticós, Industry Minister Ernesto Guevara, Labor Minister Augusto Martínez Sánchez, and Captain Antonio Núñez Jiménez . Later, at the ceremony in the cemetery, the photographer Alberto Díaz ("Korda") took the photograph of Che which was to become one of the most famous of all time, and which he was to title "The Heroic Guerrilla."

I have never considered myself an economist, but rather a functionary of the Cuban government, as just another Cuban

In 1960 two television programs—"People's University" and "Face the Press"—were launched, with the aim of informing the population on national and international events. Members of the Revolutionary leadership participated in these programs, together with a panel of journalists. Che was a regular participant.

GUEVARA

GUEVARA

The United States has for some time been preparing an attack against the Cuban people and was ready to launch it, but President Nikita Khruschev made its plans public... The most logical thing to expect now is the intensification of the economic blockade again Cuba.

Previous page and Below: **Moscow, October and November 1960**

Che visited the Soviet Union three times during a two-month trip to the countries of the Soviet Bloc and China in 1960. He first met with Soviet President Nikita Khruschev in October (below) and visited Moscow's Red Square and the Lenin Mausoleum with Cuban ambassador Faure Chomón in November (previous page, on his right).

Above: **With Mao Tse-Tung, China, December 1960**

Che was received in China by President Mao Tse-Tung at an official ceremony in the Government Palace. Che wanted to see for himself what the experience of the Chinese Revolution had to offer a country struggling to establish some measure of economic independence. He was offered $60 million of credits with which to purchase an industrial plant from China.

Our efforts are focused on the push for unity amongst the world's underdeveloped nations in order to present a coherent front

Above: **Che with Ahmed Sukarno, Havana, 11th May 1960**

Che visited Indonesia in 1959 and President Sukarno visited
Havana the following year.

Above: **Santiago de Cuba, 1960**

Visiting the home in Santiago de Cuba of a fighter in the Rebel Army, with Aleida.

Below: **Police Academy, Havana, 1960**

Che with Efigenio Ameijeiras, the head of police during the early
years of the Revolution, taking part in the graduation ceremony
for the first course held by the Havana Police Academy.

I went to pick up the order of the day from Che and found him smoking a cigar about a foot and a half long made by some admirers among the Havana tobacco workers. With a roguish smile he told me: "Don't worry about the doctors. I'm obeying their orders—just one cigar a day, no more no less."

Recollection of Che's secretary at the time, Antonio Núñez Jiménez

We are face to face with history and quite simply we must not be afraid! We must maintain the same enthusiasm and faith that we have up to now.

Left: **In conversation, Santiago de Cuba, 1961**

Che is met at the airport by Manuel Piñeiro (known as "Redbeard"), who was to become a member of the Central Committee of the Communist Party of Cuba. At this time he was military chief in Santiago de Cuba, with his headquarters in the Moncada Barracks. After Che's death in Bolivia in 1967, Piñeiro played a key role in reconstructing the history of Che's internationalist activities.

Che on moral incentives

To construct communism the new man has to be created as well as the material base. At times of extreme danger it is easy to promote moral incentives; to maintain their force, it is necessary to develop a consciousness whereby new values are acquired and society as a whole is transformed into one enormous school.

Left: **Tribute, Electricity Company, Havana, 8th May 1961**

Speaking at a ceremony in memory of the anti-imperialist leader Antonio Guiteras.

Voluntary work becomes a means of bonding and understanding between our workers

Above and Right: **Voluntary work in Havana Port, 1961**

Che believed in setting an example at all times, and so after he finished his working day as a minister, and at weekends, he would often undertake manual tasks—as here, where he is loading sacks of sugar in Havana Port with Orlando Borrego, who worked with him in the Ministry of Industry. Borrego later published Che's writings and speeches in a limited edition of seven volumes.

224

To reach the people you have to feel one of them, you have to know what they want, what they need

Left: **Building schools, Havana, 1961**

From the beginning it was decided to bring education to every corner of the country, and a school building program was initiated. Che is here participating in the construction of a primary school.

Above: **The minister and the workers, Havana, March 1961**

Che required rigorous discipline, from himself and others, but at the same time could be informal and intimate.

Left: **Havana, February 1961**

Drinking from a communal mug during the construction of housing in eastern Havana.

He is the most fascinating and most dangerous member of the Triumvirate. He has a sweet and melancholy smile that many women find quite devastating. Che is steering Cuba with a coldly calculating mind, exceptional competence, exceptional intelligence, and a great sense of humor.

Time magazine, 8th August 1960

Left: **Listening to Fidel, Havana, 1961**

Fidel Castro had just returned from a visit to the Soviet Union.

Letter to his parents
Passion is needed for any great work, and for the Revolution passion and audacity are required in big doses

When he spoke Che would gesticulate little, if at all. He spoke sparingly and was never one for long speeches. Even so, the consistency of his arguments held the attention of his listeners.

★ Punta del Este conference

We were attending this conference so that the peoples may move towards a happy future, of harmonious development, so that they are not converted into appendices of imperialism in preparation for a new and terrible war

At the Punta del Este conference in Uruguay the administration of US President John F Kennedy unveiled its **Alliance for Progress**, an aid package for Latin America intended to counter communism. Che attacked the US scheme as "**financial bribery**," and claimed that Cuba offered a better model for economic development. At a party after the conference he met Kennedy's aide Richard Goodwin who, in his report to Kennedy, later wrote of Che: "behind the beard **his features are quite soft**, almost feminine, and his **manner is intense**. He has a good sense of humor, and there was considerable joking back and forth ... He spoke calmly, in a straightforward manner, and with the appearance of detachment and objectivity."

According to Goodwin, Che said that Cuba would like a modus vivendi with the United States, and could discuss paying for expropriated US property through trade. Che thanked the United States for its failed **Bay of Pigs** invasion four months earlier—"it had been a **great political victory** for them—enabled them to consolidate—and transformed them from an aggrieved little country to an equal."

Above: **Journey to Punta del Este, Havana, 2nd August 1961**

Che chats with Fidel Castro and Captain Antonio Núñez Jiménez
at Havana airport, before leaving for Punta del Este in Uruguay
where he led the Cuban delegation at the economic conference
of the Organization of American States.

Left: **Che's family, Punta del Este, Uruguay, 1961**

Che's Argentinian family and old friends took the opportunity to visit him during the Organization of American States conference. From left to right, Ana María Guevara; Juan Martín, the youngest brother, his father Don Ernesto; and his brother Roberto Guevara.

★ Bay of Pigs
Cuban Missile Crisis
Patria o muerte!

The new US administration of **John F Kennedy** lost little time in completing the plans inherited from President Eisenhower for an invasion of Cuba. The idea of a socialist country 90 miles from the Florida coast, allied with the Soviet Union, and which had nationalized one billion dollars of US assets, was too much for the North American politicians to stomach. Washington found willing recruits for an invasion among the Cubans who had left to establish themselves in Miami.

The **CIA** infiltrated 35 agents into Cuba to organize sabotage and prepare a guerrilla campaign. At least one was a double agent, and the Cuban government was well aware of US plans.

On 14th April 1961 one of the CIA groups burned down the luxury Havana department store El Encanto, causing the death of an employee, and the next morning US planes bombed Cuban airfields and destroyed most of the country's small air force. At the funeral for the victims the following day Fidel Castro publicly announced that Cuba's **revolution was socialist** for the first time.

During the night of 17th April the 1,500 men of the exile "Liberation Army" landed at Playa Girón on the **Bay of Pigs**, on Cuba's south coast to the west of Cienfuegos. Within hours the Cuban armed forces, led personally by **Fidel Castro**, had the invaders pinned down and launched their attack. President Kennedy had miscalculated and failed to provide air cover, for which the Cuban exiles would never forgive him. After three days 114 invaders were dead, and nearly **1,300 taken prisoner**. They were to be sent back to the United States later in exchange for $62 million of medicines and baby food.

Che spent the days of the invasion with the western army guarding Pinar del Río province. Although he did not see action, he came within an inch of death when he dropped his pistol and the bullet from it grazed his head.

In response to the failed invasion, and a new wave of terrorist attacks on the island sponsored by the CIA, the Cuban government stepped up its overtures to the Soviet Union, seeking weapons as well as economic and technical support.

On 16th October 1962 Kennedy received proof in the form of aerial photographs that **Soviet atomic missiles** had been installed in Cuba. The days that followed, which became known as the Cuban Missile Crisis, brought the world to the brink of nuclear war. Kennedy demanded the withdrawal of the missiles, and on 29th October Soviet **President Nikita Khruschev** agreed—in exchange for withdrawal of US missiles from Turkey on the Soviet Union's southern border.

Fidel Castro and Che were furious. The Cuban leadership had been prepared to stare down the threat of US attack even if it had involved the world in nuclear conflagration.

Above: **Return from Moscow, Havana airport, 6th September 1962**

Che had gone to the Soviet Union ostensibly to discuss industrial development, but with a broader brief to win from the Soviets a commitment to defend Cuba in the event of another attack by the United States. The Soviet build-up of missiles in Cuba was well under way, and Che discussed with Soviet President Khruschev a military cooperation and defence agreement. But Khruschev did not sign the agreement, and Che returned to Cuba with only verbal assurances.

The Soviet Union, making use of its sovereignty, can, if it feels like annoying the United States, sell us oil and buy sugar from us to annoy the United States. But what do we care?

Following page: **Che and Fidel, Havana, 1962**

After the Missile Crisis of October 1962, Soviet President Nikita Khruschev invited Fidel Castro to Moscow, with the aim of smoothing over Cuban ill-feelings at the withdrawal of Soviet nuclear missiles from Cuba without prior consultation. On his return to Cuba, Castro gave a televised broadcast to explain the outcome of his trip. Here he is in discussion with Che in the television studio before his speech.

We have converted the fortresses into schools

Below: **"We Have Won!" end of the Year of Literacy, Revolution Square, Havana, 22nd December 1961**

Che looks on from the tribune as Fidel Castro declares that Cuba has become an "Illiteracy Free Territory." Over the past year the Literacy Campaign had sent tens of thousands of volunteer teachers throughout the island, with the result that 979,506 people—out of a population of 5 million—learned to read and write for the first time. The end of the campaign was celebrated with a huge demonstration in Havana.

Above: **Rafael Enríquez, 1987**

Che on his personal work ethic

CHE: Hey, comrade, where's your machete?

DRIVER: I'm not here to cut. I'm the driver.

CHE: Look, anyone can be a driver: find a machete and get to work like everyone else, or leave right now. And don't worry about the truck—if I have to, I'll drive back myself.

Left: **The cane field, 1962**

The struggle to increase sugar production was to attract the participation of a huge part of the Cuban population in the so-called "People's Harvests." The Revolutionary Leadership and visiting foreigners helped alongside the peasants. Here Che is framed by sugar cane.

Above and Left: **Industry Minister, Havana, May 1962**

Che's style was to create an immediate and intimate bond with his audience.

Above: **Gaucho, Jovellanos, Matanzas, 1962**

Che named this thoroughbred Gaucho. Here he rides around the Ciro Redondo Farm, located in the municipality of Jovellanos in Matanzas Province. The farm constituted an experimental project based on self-sufficient agricultural production and was staffed by workers chosen by Che to cultivate vegetables, raise animals and produce leather goods and other basic products.

Right: **Che and Aleida, Pinar del Río, 1962**

Returning to the city, accompanied by Aleida, after a tour of factories and new projects.

I am neither Christ nor philanthropist ... I am the complete opposite of a Christ ... I fight with whatever arms I have at hand for what I believe in, and I try to destroy my opponent rather than letting myself be nailed to a cross or anywhere else

Left: **Havana University, 1962**

Above: **The New Man, Havana, 20th October 1962**

Che would often engage in debate with students. He wrote a lot about what he called the "New Man," whose role was to create the new society made possible by the Revolution.

Che on youth

We have been given the responsibility of leading a country during very difficult times and all that ages you, naturally it takes its toll ... But our work would not be complete if we did not know when to step down at the right time. One of your other duties is to create the people to replace us.

Above: **Comrades, Havana, 1963**

Che, who had no great love of office routine, clearly enjoyed joining in with the workers when he got the chance. Here he is on a visit to the Ñico López sugar refinery, one of the country's most important and a place he visited frequently during his years as Industry Minister.

Right: **Albert Kuntz Factory, Havana, 3rd January 1962**

The development of a national industrial infrastructure was a priority of the new government. As part of the plans for economic co-operation between the two countries Che, in his role as Industry Minister, inaugurated this cookie factory in the company of the Ambassador of the German Democratic Republic.

This generation which has made possible the apparent miracle of a socialist revolution in the backyard of North American imperialism has to pay for the glory with its sacrifice

Left: **Havana University, 11th May 1962**

At a ceremony in the main auditorium of Havana University, Che met with students to discuss the importance of technical studies for industrial progress.

I don't drink, I smoke. I would cease to be a man if I didn't like women; I would cease to be a revolutionary if for this or that reason I did not fulfill my revolutionary duties to the end.

Right: **Confessions, Havana, 28th June 1962**

Interview with
Doctor Oscar Fernández Mel

Above: **Oscar Fernández Mel (on right)**

Born in Colón, Matanzas province. He qualified as an orthopedic doctor and joined the guerrillas in the Sierra Maestra as a doctor. He was a member of Che's Column 8 which cut the island in two with its victory in the battle of Santa Clara. After the Revolution he was with Che in the Cabaña fortress in Havana. During the Bay of Pigs invasion he was head of the medical services of the Revolutionary Armed Forces. Later he served as Mayor of Havana and Ambassador in London. Currently retired from the armed forces, he continues to work as a doctor.

Interview in Havana, January 2003

For me the aspect of Che that I most like to talk about is Che after the triumph of the Revolution, when he emerges as a statesman, a man of action, the man who is required to become an economist, who is required to become Industry Minister and becomes Industry Minister.

He would meet engineers, metallurgists in order to talk about their subject; and he would do so fluently, almost as if giving a speech, thanks to his calling and above all to his devotion to the matter in hand. He was also a writer, journalist, founder of the *Verde Olivo* (*Olive Green*) newspaper in which he would first appear in print, as well as being the author of articles in various prestigious national and international publications. A man of many facets but with a single goal. He was the man who would represent Cuba in all kinds of international gatherings, the man tasked with overseas responsibilities, the man who was to speak up for Cuba and its Revolution.

He was a well-educated man, possibly one of the Revolution's best-educated; not that he was one to brag about it. He could express an opinion or point of view on just about everything in the course of a conversation, be it from the historical or philosophical as well as the literary perspective.

He was very fond of good poetry and tried writing some himself, such as the verses dedicated to San Luis on the occasion of his passing away. He dabbled in poetry, the truth is he liked to write but with so much work he was unable to spend much time on things that he enjoyed doing. He also admired the Mexican poet León Felipe.

He was keen on the arts, ballet; and in spite of being an amateur he never failed to appreciate it as an expression of physical beauty: good music, although he had no ear for music, completely tone deaf. He danced an awful tango, he tried to hum them but he would be out of tune. And as for dancing … Alberto Granado, his friend from Córdoba, has a few tales to tell. He used to say to him: "Hey! When they play something that you know I can dance to tell me …" and they would play one thing and he would get up and dance to another.

He was an indefatigable critic, he loved art. He would visit the museums in all the towns he would be in; and was well-versed in humanity's foremost achievements.

He was no stranger to the cultural scene. He could talk about any historical figure or any facet of culture. He would talk about Franz Kafka as if he had been an acquaintance … and when he told a story he did it very well. He would always try to find time to increase the knowledge that he had begun to acquire as a child, thanks to his mother. She was a charming woman, very erudite and intelligent and with whom you could talk for hours. She had an exquisite sweetness in her expression which must have softened her character. He worshipped his mother.

Che was a photographer, as everyone knows. He earned a living from photography while in Mexico. He loved to take photos. Currently his camera, with a 1.1 lens, is kept in La Cabaña Fortress in Havana. He bought this camera when he arrived in the capital, in the first years of the Revolution. Later on his workload wouldn't allow him to take a lot of photos. At one time he was about to give away his Nikon. I said to him: "Look, Che. Don't do away with your camera. Here, have this!" And I gave him my Kiev, a really good camera that I had been given in the Soviet Union. So two or three days later he sent me his Nikon: and I keep it as a unique memento, preserved there, in La Cabaña.

He knew about the finer things in life, but didn't indulge in them. That's not to say that he didn't admire them, nor that he rejected them. He just didn't chase after them. He would admire a good painting, a good piece of jewelry, a good timepiece. He was fairly liberal with his spending and was no hair-shirted professional proletarian, but renounced material goods in the cause of social justice.

The clothes that he wore have been talked about, criticizing how he went about it as if he hadn't a clue about how to wear a decent suit, to appear well-dressed. I could never have remotely conceived of him turning up at the Ministry in collar and tie. He sought out comfort and the freshness of feeling free. The olive-green combat uniform that he would so often wear was made of a very breathable cotton fabric and it made him feel really good. He wouldn't tuck in his shirt and the boots that he wore were those made by the Industry Ministry. Often he would give them to one of his aides to break them in for him, then wear them himself. Although more comfortable boots were offered to him, paratroopers' boots made of calfskin, he never wore them. He appreciated the gesture but wouldn't accept them.

At other times he gave the impression of being brusque, although Che was a very polite man. He was perfectly versed in social and moral etiquette and knew how to employ them. He wasn't the impudent type. Many stories have been told about him which do not accurately reflect how he was.

This "other" Che, exceptional guerrilla fighter, statesman, revolutionary, well-educated, lover of poetry and good music, austere, self-critical; who loved his children, wife, and family; who would enjoy a good roast or perhaps a good wine when circumstances permitted. Nevertheless he was no drinker and still less a Bohemian type.

For him, honor was the foundation stone of his life. Everything he did he did on behalf of and in honor of the Revolution. Moreover, what scared him more than anything else was upsetting the Revolutionary Movement.

I could see how he developed from his earliest speeches. I remember the first that he gave in front of a group of peasants in El Pedrero, up there in the Escambray, in the heart of the island. He went so far as to make some surrealist references. It was too ideological for his audience. I thought the words were fine; they weren't too long but they weren't well understood by that audience.

Later Che would start to be an orator. In his speeches he would be very sparing, expressing ideas very tersely. Sometimes I would be watching television when he would come up and say to me: "You can't just read out, you have to improvize." He would start off talking for ten minutes and then would say: "'Today I spoke for 15 minutes. The thing developed and I was speaking for half an hour." He was never one for lengthy speeches, yet he did express everything that he had to say in a co-ordinated fashion and which appealed to people in spite of his linear approach during his speeches. He would gesticulate little, if at all.

His speeches contained several of his strengths—his honesty, one of those that I admire the most—and his way of being aware that one should do as one says.

He never said one thing to your face and then another behind your back. He was scrupulous in this in his personal and private, as well as his public, life.

His honesty would withstand any test. At times his criticisms and way of thinking could be hurtful, but that was the way he was. He was not interested in life's material benefits, not even in food or comforts. For him these were insignificant things.

When we were in the Congo and could see that things weren't working out, that there was no way of sorting it out, he tried to get things moving. His primary concern was the reputation of the Cuban Revolution. Where would it leave the Cuban Revolution if we were to get out after leaving behind a failure? I believe that this formed part of the honor that he took such great care of: but not a petulant sense of honor, rather a sincere honour, of doing the right thing for the good of society and the good of humanity.

His life revolved around the Revolution, his concern for humanity and the struggle for the welfare of all. His beliefs were leading him to the concept of the New Man in a generic fashion: that is to say to the transformation of thoughts into the actions and deeds of a different kind of society. We do not know when this will come about, but he was a proponent of these ideas.

It is a shame that he died. Given his age and the political, cultural, social, and historical changes that were taking place he could have played a much more practical role on behalf of the Revolution and Cuba.

He always said that he had to leave something to remember him by, something with which humanity would be reminded of him; and he's managed it in abundance yet without any arrogance whatsoever. He's achieved it to the extent that 35 years after his death he is talked about more than when he died. There are more than 70 books about Che; around ten biographies each of more than 800 pages by important writers exist. There is something about his image. The Mexican writer and novelist Paco Ignacio Taibo, Junior, when asked about what it is that goes to make up the magic of that image of Che which can constantly be seen all over the world; displayed by people who don't even know who he is, let alone where Cuba is nor where Bolivia is, says something on the lines of: "…his image is the manifestation of a transparency and supernatural honesty."

Above: **The vanguard, Havana, June 1962**

Che was a strong advocate of "moral incentives" as a way of encouraging workers to work harder through "socialist emulation." Each month there would be a meeting in the Ministry of Industry when Che would present certificates to distinguished workers.

Right: **Cement factory, Artemisa, Pinar del Río, 1964**

During a break in one of his days of voluntary labor, Che shares ideas and experiences with workers in a cement factory. He advocated that work should be embraced as "meaningful play," providing a source of happiness for the "New Man."

Above: **Argentinians together, Camagüey, 1962**

Cutting cane by hand is one of the hardest agricultural tasks.
Here, Che is with his old Argentinian friend Alberto Granado.
They are accompanied by Aleida March.

Above and Right: **Playing chess, Havana**

After the Revolution, Che's fondness for chess was rekindled, and he attended most national and international tournaments held in Cuba. He played against, and sometimes beat, leading international players such as Boris de Grief (Colombia), Ren Letelier (Chile), Echeverry (Uruguay), and Carlos Bielicki (Argentina). In simultaneous games he drew with the Soviet player Mikhail Tal and with the Argentinian Miguel Najdorf.

When I left the Ministry I called my wife and told her "I am going to visit my other girlfriend" and she replied, "I know, you are going to play chess."

He preferred an aggressive game, based on audacity and combativeness

Recollection of Cuban Chess Grand Master, Eleazar Jiménez

Above: **Havana University, 1963**

Che speaking with students at Havana University about the ethical values of the Revolution, which brought profound changes in Cubans' way of thinking. The literacy campaign undertaken in 1961 and the university reforms of 1962 responded to strong popular demand for knowledge.

You have to paint
yourself as black,
as mulatto, as a
worker, as a
peasant; you have
to reach out to
the people,
because the
University is not
the preserve
of anybody.
It belongs to
the people...

Che on Che

For me CHE signifies the most essential, the most loved aspects of my own life. How could I not like it? The first and second names of a person are small things, personal, insignificant. In contrast, I like it very much when people call me CHE.

Right: **Reliving old times, Matanzas**

On one of his visits to the Ciro Redondo experimental farm in Jovellanos, Che relived old times when he traveled on his inseparable companion La Poderosa, the motorbike which accompanied him on the first journeys of his youth.

Following page: **Camilo's first birthday, Havana, May 1963**

Che and Aleida in their house in Nuevo Vedado, Havana, with their first two children, Aleidita and Camilo, and Hildita, Che's daughter by his first wife Hilda Gadea.

Above: **Casablanca, Havana, 1964**

Visiting a primary school in the Havana municipality of
Casablanca, in the eastern part of the city.

In this small Cuba, with four or five television channels, with hundreds of radio stations, with all the advances of modern science, when those children arrived at school at night for the first time and saw the electric lights, they exclaimed that the stars were very low that night

Above and Right: **Relaxing at home, Havana, 1964**

These photographs were taken in the Guevara family home,
now the Study Centre that bears his name. On the right, he is
with Aleida, his mother Celia and three of his children—Hildita,
Aleidita, and Camilo. Che spent most of his week working
through his ministerial responsibilities and on evenings and
weekends he did voluntary work. His main family time was
reserved for Sunday afternoons.

Che on love

At the risk of seeming ridiculous, let me say that the true revolutionary is guided by a great feeling of love. It is impossible to think of a genuine revolutionary lacking this quality.

282

Amongst the personal shortcomings in every man, my own are so obvious and expressed in the form of violent contradictions

Left: **Industry Minister, his office, Havana, 1964**

Because this country, Algeria, is impassioned, it will make as much noise in Africa as Cuba in the Americas

Left: **With President Ahmed Ben Bella, Algeria, April 1964**

Che was enthusiastically received in Algeria, a country which had won its independence from France just a few years before. Over the years he became a personal friend of Ben Bella. To this day one of the main boulevards in Algiers is named after him.

For a revolutionary getting to know Algeria is encouraging and stimulating

Above: **Visiting the Timgad Ruins, Algeria, April 1964**

On his visit to Algeria Che visited the ancient city of Timgad, at the foot of the Aures mountains south of Constantine. Since his youthful travels through Latin America he had been passionate about photography and also about archeology, and on his overseas travels representing the Cuban government he pursued these hobbies whenever he was able. A collection of his photographs has been curated by the Che Guevara Center in Havana.

This continent represents one of, if not the, most important battlefields against every form of exploitation that exists in the world

Left: **Ghana, January 1965**

Wearing traditional Ghanaian costume, Che attended the exhibition on Cuba organized to coincide with his visit. At the end of December 1964, he began an extensive tour of the African continent, which would have a decisive influence on his future. A year later, having taken the nom de guerre of "Tatu," he returned as a guerrilla with a group of Cubans to fight in the Congo.

What I really dislike is our lack of courage at times to face up to certain realities, sometimes economic and sometimes political. Especially economic. Sometimes we have had comrades who follow the policy of the ostrich, of hiding their head. In economic problems we have put the blame on the drought, on imperialism...

Left: **Meditations, Moscow, 1964**

Following page: **Che with Yuri Gagarin, Moscow, 11th November 1964**

At a reception organized by the Soviet government at the end of 1964 Che met Yuri Gagarin, the first man to go into space and orbit the Earth.

291

Che on patriotism
I was born in Argentina, it's no secret to anyone. I am both Cuban and Argentinian and, if it does not offend their Latin American lordships, I am as patriotic about Latin America as anyone else.

Left: **At the United Nations, New York, 1964**

Che represented Cuba in the XIX General Assembly of the United Nations which opened on 9th December.

Above: **Waiting, United Nations, New York, 1964**

In his olive-green dress uniform Che waits his turn to speak. He did not have much faith in the ability of the UN to resolve conflicts, seeing it as essentially a tool of the Great Powers, but used it as a platform to make Cuba's predicament more widely known.

Right: **Speech at the United Nations, New York, December 1964**

On 11th December Che made a historic speech at the United Nations on the situation of Cuba and the other countries of the Third World. In his reply to the discussion which followed he stated, in reference to the division of the world into power blocs, that "There are no longer small enemies or insignificant forces, because there are no longer isolated peoples."

Che on peace

Peaceful coexistence must be practiced between all states, independently of their size, of the previous historical relations between them, and of the problems that may emerge between some of them, at a given moment

And if it were said of us that we're almost romantics, that we are incorrigible idealists, that we think the impossible: then a thousand and one times we have to answer that yes, we are

Left: **Between Ourselves, Havana, 1962**

Above: **TV appearance, 1964**

Che was a natural performer in front of the television cameras, with a strong, direct delivery. He was able to move effortlessly between quoting poetry, explaining philosophical ideas, and recounting scenes from literature and from everyday life.

Left: **A passion for photography, Havana, May 1964**

Celebrating the sixth May Day since the Revolution, from the platform in Revolution Square, Che took Liborio Noval's camera to make his own record of the day. Behind him on the right of the photograph is the famous Communist leader of the Republicans in the Spanish Civil War, Dolores Ibarruri (La Pasionaria), who had been living in exile in Moscow for three decades.

299

Revolutions, accelerated radical social changes, are made of circumstances; not always, almost never, or perhaps never can science predict their mature form in all its detail. They are made of passions, of man's fight for social vindication, and are never perfect. Neither was ours.

Above: **The Interview, Camagüey, 1964**

During the sugar harvest Che is surprised by a Chilean journalist visiting Cuba at the time.

Above: **May Day, Havana, 1964**

From the podium in Revolution Square, Che observes the traditional parade to mark Workers' Day.

Above: **Revolution Square, 1964**

Che chats with Celia Sánchez. She was until her death in 1980 one of Castro's closest aides and companions.

Right: **JESÚS FORJAN, 1969**

DIA DEL GUERRILLERO HEROICO
Octobre 8
DAY OF THE HEROIC GUERRILLA FIGHTER
Octobre 8
JOURNEE DU GUERRILLERO HEROIQUE
8 Octobre

Even Che couldn't always be like Che. Sometimes he got tired, too, and got home worn out and just wanted to be with his kids.

Recollection of fellow guerrilla, Haydée Santamaría

Left and following page: **At home with his family and new baby, Celia, Havana, 1964**

Internatio

al Fighter

Chapter 4

★ Fighting imperialism in the Congo and Bolivia

If one day you must read this...

After meeting Fidel Castro, Che saw himself as **fighting for socialism** wherever he could be of use, and he repeated this often during his time in the Sierra Maestra and later as a government official in Havana. His goal was the overthrow of imperialism, which he saw as a global capitalist system which oppressed less-developed countries. Joining the struggle in Cuba was for him a phase in that struggle, which he hoped to extend to other countries in the Americas, and particularly his native Argentina.

In 1961 Che began organizing groups of revolutionaries to fight as **guerrillas on the Latin American continent**. The first to leave Cuba went to Guatemala in December of that year. At around this time hundreds of left-wing Latin Americans were arriving in Havana. Soon Cuba was assisting movements in Algeria, Nicaragua, Peru, Guatemala, Venezuela, and Argentina, with Che taking a close interest. In Argentina Che's mother Celia became actively involved in socialist politics, and spent three months in jail.

By the summer of 1964 Che had decided to leave Cuba to **return to the guerrilla struggle** himself. On 1st April the following year, disguised as a middle-aged businessman and codenamed **Ramón**, he left Cuba secretly for Tanzania and thence to the **Congo**. There he met up with 136 Cuban fighters, all but five of them of African descent, and took the name **Tatu**. The plan was to give support and training to the guerrilla forces under the command of Laurent Kabila.

As Che attested in his diaries, the experience of trying to instill discipline and develop a common ideological approach among the Congolese was an uphill struggle. After little more than six months Che, unusually filled with self-doubt and holding himself responsible for **failure**, withdrew the Cuban contingent and made his way back to Havana via Prague. "We cannot liberate by ourselves a country that does not wish to fight," he wrote.

In October 1966 Che, who had **returned to Cuba clandestinely**, left again with a Uruguayan passport in the name of Ramón Benítez. He had said goodbye to his wife and children in his new disguise and eaten dinner with them, without his children recognizing he was their father.

To avoid the attention of the CIA he flew first to Moscow, then to Prague, Paris, Madrid, and São Paolo, and from there to La Paz, the capital of **Bolivia**. On 7th November he set out with three other Cubans for an isolated farm that they had purchased. The plan this time, worked out in detail with Fidel Castro, was to establish a training center for Latin American guerrillas in the heart of South America. Bolivia was selected for its strategic location bordering Argentina, Brazil, Paraguay, Chile, and Peru.

The **Bolivian Communist Party** refused to support Che's guerrilla strategy, and in the first three months he was able to recruit only a fifth of the 250 fighters he had planned to attract. From the start the small guerrilla force was infiltrated by **informers** and suffered many **desertions**, and it was forced into combat with the Bolivian army months before it was ready. The terrain was far harsher than Cuba's Sierra Maestra, and many of the guerrillas got sick and even showed signs of malnutrition. The peasants proved suspicious of the guerrillas, and often **hostile**, leaving the guerrilla band dangerously exposed to attack.

From Che's last letter to his parents before leaving for the Congo

Dear Viejos:

Once again I feel under my heels the ribs of Rocinante,* I return to the trail with my shield on my arm...

Nothing essential is changed, except that I am much more conscious, my Marxism is rooted and principled. I believe in the armed struggle as the only solution for the peoples who fight to free themselves and I am consistent with my beliefs. Many will call me an adventurer, and I am, but of a different type, of those who put their lives on the line to demonstrate their truths.

It could be that this will be the definitive one. I don't go looking for it but it is within the logical calculation of probabilities. If it is to be, then this is my final embrace.

A kiss to Celia, to Roberto, Juan Martín and Patotín, to Beatriz, to everybody. For you, a big hug from your obstinate and prodigal son,

Ernesto

*Rocinante was Don Quixote's horse.

Above: **ORLANDO YANEZ, 1977**

Letter to Fidel

Havana, Year of Agriculture*

Fidel

At this time I am reminded of many things, of when we first met in María Antonia's house, of when you proposed that I should come along, of all the tension of the preparations.

One day they came by, asking who was to be informed in case of death and the real possibility of that hit home to all of us. Later we knew that it was true—in a Revolution you either triumph or die (if it is a real one). Many comrades were left behind on the road to victory.

Today everything has a less dramatic tone, because we are more mature, but the event repeats itself. I feel that I have fulfilled that part of my duty that tied me to the Cuban Revolution in its territory, and I say my farewells to you, to the comrades and to your people, that is now mine too.

I formally resign my positions within the leadership of the Party, of my post as Minister, my rank of Commander, my status as a Cuban citizen. Nothing legal binds me to Cuba, only ties of another kind that cannot be broken as official appointments can.

Recalling my past life, I believe that I have labored with enough honor and dedication to consolidate the revolutionary triumph. My only failing of any importance was not to have had more confidence in you from the first moments in the Sierra Maestra and not to have understood soon enough your abilities as a leader and a revolutionary. I have lived magnificent days, and felt at your side the pride of belonging to our people in the brilliant yet sad days of the Caribbean Crisis.

Seldom has a statesman shone as brightly as you did in those days. I also take pride in having followed you without hesitation, identifying with your way of thinking and seeing and understanding the dangers and principles.

Other lands call for my modest efforts. I can do that which your duties at the forefront of Cuba deny you, and the time for us to separate has arrived.

Let it be known that I undertake this with a mixture of joy and sorrow; I am leaving behind the purest of my hopes as a builder and the dearest among those I love … and I leave behind a people that took me in as a son. That wounds a part of my spirit. I carry to new battlefields the faith that you instilled in me, the revolutionary spirit of my people, the feeling of fulfilling the most sacred of duties: to fight against imperialism wherever it may be. This comforts and heals the deepest of wounds.

I will just say that I free Cuba of any responsibility except that which stems from its example. If my hour of reckoning comes beneath other skies, my last thought will be of this people and of you. I thank you for your teachings and your example to which I will endeavour to be faithful up to the final consequences of my deeds. I have always been identified with the foreign policy of our revolution and continue to be so. Wherever I may end up I will feel the responsibility of what it means to be a Cuban revolutionary, and as such I will behave. To my wife and children I leave nothing material and that does not sadden me. I am happy for it to be so. I ask for nothing for them as the State will provide for them to live and be educated.

I would have so much to say to you and our people, but I feel they are unnecessary, words cannot express what I would want them to, and it isn't worth filling more sheets of paper.

Forever onwards to victory!

Fatherland or death!

I embrace you with all revolutionary fervor.

Che

* From 1959 the government gave a name to each year with reference to a special goal or to commemorate some event in Cuban history. 1965 was denoted the "Year of Agriculture."

Above: **Victory, Havana, 1959**

If imperialism is still around we will go out and fight it; if it is finished you (Ernestito), Camilo, and I can take a vacation on the moon

Right: **Father, Havana, 1965**

One of the last photos of Che with his four children by his second marriage, Camilo, Celia, Aleidita, and the newly born Ernestito. A few days later Che began a new clandestine life, leaving for the Congo on 1st April.

Above: **Departure, Havana, March 1965**

This and the following photographs are the last of Che and Fidel Castro together before Che's departure for the Congo.

I had left behind almost 11 years of work for the Cuban Revolution at Fidel's side, a happy home—to the extent one can call the house where a revolutionary dedicated to his work lives—and a bunch of kids who barely knew of my love. The cycle was beginning again.

I took just two small keepsakes with me to the struggle, the wound dressing from my wife and the key ring with the stone, from my mother

Above: **The departure, Havana, March 1965**

Interview with Colonel Víctor Dreke

Above: **Víctor Dreke**

Born in Sagua la Grande. He was one of the leaders of the General Strike of
9th April 1958, and later joined the Directorio Estudiantil (Student
Directorate) operating in the towns. He ended the revolutionary war as a
Comandante of the Directorio. He was selected as the official Head of
Mission of Che's group of military advisers in the Congo. He is currently a
retired colonel of the Revolutionary Armed Forces.

Interview in Havana, 25th January 2002

I had a wonderful experience with Che in Africa. I first had the chance to get to know him in October 1958, when he arrived at the head of his guerrilla column in the mountainous Escambray massif, located in the center of the island of Cuba. I had been wounded, and without knowing me, Che came up and immediately took an interest in my injuries. He lifted my spirits by saying to me that I would soon be able to go back to the fighting as my wound wasn't serious. His words were a combination of strength and kindness. At that time I had no idea that I would be fighting alongside him in other lands, as he himself was to write in his farewell letter to Fidel, just before he left for the place where my ancestors were born—Africa.

The second time I met him was on the night of 31st March 1965, seven years later. On that day I had the privilege to be one of the first Cubans to set eyes upon Che transformed into Ramón Benítez, the false identity he assumed when he left Cuba on 1st April that year.

What was it that led up to such a moving encounter that night? I found myself in a training camp where we were preparing ourselves for the Congo. I was to be head of the column. Osmany Cienfuegos came up and he said to me: "There's a commander called Ramón who says he knows you, that he's a friend of yours. He'll be joining the ranks. He shows me the photos of this commander. I look at them and say to him 'I don't know him.' "

A few days later Osmany came back with the news that I was to get ready to leave camp. It had been decided that I was no longer to be head of the column, but that from now on Ramón was in charge. I went along with this: I just said to him that all I wanted to do was go.

The next day I was transferred to a house in Havana. I couldn't imagine what was about to happen there. It was an emotional night. Something I will never forget. Even today, I remember it with disbelief.

We get to the house and Osmany introduces me to José María Martínez Tamayo, known as "Papi" amongst the Bolivian guerrillas. I look around and some distance away I saw a comrade sat at a table writing and tearing up sheets of paper. I have no idea who he is. I'm watching him writing and tearing up paper. I say hello. The man doesn't respond. I stay sitting with Osmany.

Not long after, Osmany goes over to this person, they talk and call me over.

Osmany says to me: "Anyway, Víctor, this is Commander Ramón. He's going to lead the column."

I stop and greet him. He returns my greeting but doesn't say anything to me. And I look at him time and again, to see if I know him. I don't know … Spanish or something similar … I don't know him. And he's still silent. Osmany is laughing, until at last the person says: "Osmany! Stop pissing around. Víctor, I'm Che."

That's how it was, something I can't describe even today. It was the most important moment in my life! I can't compare it to anything else that's happened. I didn't know what to do. All sorts of things came into my head. Now serious, Osmany says to me: "It's been decided by the Commander-in-Chief and Raúl that on his journey he'll be accompanied by you and Papi."

I can tell you in all honesty that even now I'm thrilled when I think of that moment. For the faith in me held by Fidel, Raúl, and Che, who of course agreed that we two were to accompany him.

In Papi's case, he already knew him due to the two having worked together for a long time. They had been together when preparing the struggle in Argentina. Their internationalist and revolutionary activities had brought them together, as well as their bravery, craftiness, and boldness. Papi was a very courageous young man.

At that time I wasn't a friend of Che's. I had met him in October 1958, and had been with him on a few occasions since: but I couldn't say that we were friends, not like he was with Papi. That's why I was so thrilled with the opportunity that my life had put before me. Moreover, it would have been just as easy to have chosen another comrade. There are so many Cubans who, thanks to their bravery and their contributions to the Revolution, could have been chosen to accompany him. But it fell to me, and truly, it was a privilege.

Che was unique; and his teachings and the example he set remain entrenched in many of us who were by his side.

That very night, not long after, Fidel arrived. They went off and started talking. They spent hours in conversation in an atmosphere in which it was obvious that there was real warmth and friendship between them. In my opinion, this last meeting of the two would have been similar to the first in Mexico in 1956, when Fidel convinced him of his dream of liberating Cuba. I remember that on that occasion Che had explained to his new friend that once Cuba was free some day he would depart for other countries to continue with the struggle for freedom: something that Che's detractors never talk about. Now it was the dream of brotherhood and solidarity in assisting the liberation movement in Africa, in particular in the Congo. It was at that moment that Che handed Fidel the farewell letter that he had been writing.

When we left both Papi and myself were well aware that we were answerable with Che's life. Fidel didn't say as much, but we knew. It was implicit. There was no need to say so, and without doubt it was from then on that a friendship began to be formed that was to be strengthened during seven months of the adversities and vicissitudes generated by war; and, moreover, in a territory completely unknown to Cubans. A friendship was born along with, for me, a new leader: Commander Ernesto "Che" Guevara.

Wherever we found ourselves we never left Che's side. We were well aware of our duty; and that we had to defend him, if needs be, with our lives. No argument. Then during all the time he was missing, the enemy endlessly said outrageous things; and still do so in an attempt to undermine the friendship and love that always existed between Fidel and Che.

Just imagine how many awful things would have been said if he had died before achieving his goal. How can we prove that the Revolution didn't kill him? There's no means of showing it. Moreover, the members of our column only found out it was Che when he turned up at camp. No one knew.

The route to the final objective was an extremely dangerous and complicated route. We could see Che's bravery, his concern for our comrades and above all the Congolese. He would criticize himself first, followed by the Cubans. It was only at the end of the conflict that he adopted a critical position with regard to the Africans. He thought that we, the Cubans, were better prepared than the Congolese and from the outset should have been more capable of understanding the difficulties of war.

Che was a very humane leader, able in any situation to understand how to behave in front of soldiers: how to understand men with all their shortcomings as well as virtues, their bravery as well as fear, as circumstances dictated. Some comrades thought about returning to Cuba. He told them that they couldn't go before a set time as no risks could be taken. They then asked to stay and fight, asking for their weapons and without any ill-feeling whatsoever, he handed them over. Later, these comrades would fulfill various missions. There, too, his leadership was evident.

I have countless reasons to say that Che was more than just my leader in the Congo. He was my teacher, a loyal comrade.

If I am asked whether Che thought of me as a friend, or indeed whether I myself considered him a friend: I would reply by saying that he had a very high opinion of me. He held me in esteem and above our other comrades, along with Papi.

In his diary, some of which remains unpublished, he sets out his analysis of the effectiveness of the 125 comrades who made up our column, himself included. He's extraordinarily self-critical, blaming himself for things that were not really his fault. In the diary he expresses a positive opinion about me. I hardly ever talk about it, as he speaks highly of me. This has resulted in my lifelong devotion to the Revolution, as it's not easy for Che not to make his mark on you.

He was my leader and at the end of the day I consider him a great friend. People might say: "Friends with someone after seven months?" But these were seven months of fighting together, eating together, marching together, leaving Cuba together, the three of us. I felt as close to Che as I did to Papi.

We were a threesome who were smuggled out of Cuba. Papi and myself were both aware that if the enemy found out he would be murdered or would vanish. Our duty was to accompany him and it was our responsibility to take him as far as the Congo. Later on, a group of comrades would arrive whose sole duty was to take care of his safety. Amongst them were Harry Villegas ("Pombo") and Carlos Coello ("Tuma" or "Tumaini"). That reassured us.

For me it was a once in a lifetime gift to have been able to have shared those seven months with Che. One of the many lessons I learned was to strengthen one's character in the face of adversity.

I remember when Che received the news of the death of his mother. The enemy, in a grotesque fashion, has attacked Che's feelings. They have tried to twist his sensitivity, or as they would have you believe, his lack of sensitivity in the face of such agony. Not even with that did they have any dignity.

We were in the countryside when he found out about his mother's illness, she had already fallen gravely ill. He said to me: "I'm sure that by the time this news has arrived she must be dead. There's nothing I can do." The pain was clear in his face, in spite of his strength. He was always very close to his mother. I saw him crying. His reaction to such news was logical. Personally, for me, this was an education.

In 1967, while I was at the head of our troops in Guinea-Bissau, a telegram arrived for me from Commander-in-Chief Fidel Castro which said that my mum was very ill. She had suffered an attack of thrombosis. Fidel suggested to me that if I decided to I could go back to Cuba. According to the telegram, my mum only had a few days to live. It wasn't possible for me to go—at that very moment we were in the middle of an offensive mounted by Portuguese troops; and, moreover, if I'm honest I thought of Che.

Notes

José M. Martínez Tamayo: fought alongside Che in the Sierra Maestra, in the Congolese guerrilla movement (as "Mbili"), and in the Bolivian guerrilla movement (as "Papi"). Died in combat in Bolivia, 30th July 1967.

Harry Villegas ("Pombo"): member of the Rebel Army, Che's bodyguard, fought in the Congo and later in the Bolivian guerrilla movement, which he survived. Currently holds the rank of General in the Revolutionary Armed Forces.

Carlos Coello ("Tuma"): member of the Rebel Army, Che's bodyguard and fought with him in the Congo and later Bolivia. Died in combat, 26th June 1967. In his diary, Che wrote: "In him I have lost an inseparable comrade of the last few years. He was wholly loyal. I feel his absence almost as strongly as if I had lost a son or daughter."

Osmany Cienfuegos: brother of Camilo. Later served as a member of the Council of State and, during the 1990s, as Tourism Minister.

Right: **LAZANO ABREU, "Che's America," 1970, Casa de las Américas collection**

Dia del Guerrillero Heroico 8 de octubre   Day of the Heroic Guerrilla October 8
Journée du Guérillero Héroïque 8 octobre

Left: **Combatants, Tanzania, April 1965**

From Dar-Es-Salaam to Kigoma in Tanzania is a distance of more than 1,100 miles. This photograph was taken during this long journey, made from 20 to 22 April. The group which made it were the first 13 Cubans to fight overseas after the Revolution. Che is in disguise in the white hat on the left.

My two greatest weaknesses were satisfied in the Congo: tobacco, which I was hardly ever without, and reading material, which was always abundant

Right: **The Stone, Congo, 1965**

Che's time in the Congo was full of uncertainty: the difficult situation of the war, his precarious health and the death of his mother tested Che's resolve. Even so, he continued to make time for reading and kept up his diaries. He wrote an intimate meditation on loss, which he called *The Stone* after the key ring with a stone which his mother gave him before he went away. His *Congo Diaries*, which were later published, are a deeply moving and self-critical account of this period in his life.

Following page: **Congo, 1965**

At the base camp in the Congo Che poses with three Congolese. On the second from left is Dihur Godefroid, a journalist and Che's guide.

I've learnt in the Congo that there are mistakes that I will never commit again, along with others that perhaps will occur again together with new ones... My own responsibility is great. I will never forget the defeat nor its most valuable lessons.

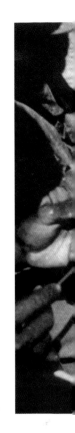

Above: **The return, Lake Tanganyika, The Congo, 1965**

On 18th November 1965 Che sent a message from his
operational base in the Congo: "The situation is collapsing. Entire
companies and peasants are going over to the enemy. There are
no reliable Congolese troops." This photograph was taken three
days later by one of the Cuban combatants while crossing Lake
Tanganyika in the direction of Tanzania. This was the end of
Che's failed intervention in the Congo.

Interview with
Ulises Estrada Lescaille

Above: **Ulises Estrada Lescaille (in foreground)**
Born in Havana. He was entrusted with the task of bringing Che back from his mission in the Congo, via Tanzania and Prague. He has worked as a journalist and in various political posts. He is currently Director of Tricontinental, the magazine of the Organization for Solidarity Among the Peoples of Asia, Africa and Latin America, founded in 1967.

Havana, 22nd January 2003

Every dawn brings a new day, and often it can be an event that gives us a pointer for the rest of our lives. That's what happened to me in December 1965, when I was assigned to go to Tanzania, with the mission of bringing Che back to Cuba. The decision was based on the black color of my skin.

On arriving in Dar-es-Salaam I met Che, who was staying in our embassy, under the strictest security measures and protected by Cuban Intelligence. You could sense the air of curiosity amongst all the Cuban and African employees, who wanted to know what was going on on the top floor of the embassy. That was instrumental in the decision to get Che out of the country quickly. Then a plan had to be drawn up, part of which meant that Che had to change his appearance. Immediately Doctor Luis García Gutiérrez, known as Fisín, was sent from the Interior Ministry; to make the false teeth and other make-up items which would form the disguise. I came back to Cuba with some photos of the transformation in his appearance together with a report written by myself and Che which contained an update on everything that had happened up to that point together with alterations to the plan to get out of Tanzania. In Cuba, Fidel Castro and Manuel Piñeiro (known as Barba Roja, or Redbeard), the Chief of Intelligence, had already been put in charge of going over and subsequently approving it. At the beginning of January 1966 I returned to Dar-es-Salaam and towards the end of the month I left for Prague along with Che, stopping over in Cairo and Yugoslavia.

From that moment the times that I spent with Che are unforgettable for me. It is a tenet of military life that whenever two people are required to complete a mission, one has to be in charge. In this case, perhaps as one of life's little ironies, Che designated me as his commander.

I remember the day of our departure. We were accompanied to Dar-es-Salaam airport by a Cuban diplomat. For security reasons this colleague left us to sort out the arrangements along the way to avoid Che spending too long waiting with other people. We were the last to board the plane. On boarding, Che sat next to the window and I next to the aisle, by chance alongside the Political Commissar of the Zanzibar Army. He began to tell me about the rumors circulating that Che was in Africa and the unfolding of the revolutionary struggle on the African continent. We were both poised for something to happen, thoughts were rushing through my head. For his part Che shrank into his seat, burying his face in the book he was reading. We went on to Cairo for a 36-hour stopover prior to Prague, our final destination.

The Cuban Embassy's commercial counsellor was waiting for us in Cairo. He had been briefed on the security measures required to ensure that our visit was absolutely secret. Of course he was supposed to have no idea that the person with me was Che! Obviously when Arbezú spoke to "Ramón" he recognized straight away that it was Che. After chatting for a while Abezú mentioned to Che that at a nearby cinema a documentary about the Tokyo Olympics was being shown, in which Enrique Figuerola, a distinguished Cuban sportsman who had won the silver medal in the 100 meters, made an appearance. Che, inspired with the sense of victory, disappeared from my sight. When I realized he was gone I immediately went to find him in the cinema and bring him back to the apartment. He understood, of course, that he had committed a reckless mistake which undermined all the security measures that had been undertaken. The next day, during the hours of darkness, we went on to Belgrade, Yugoslavia.

In Prague we were met by the head of Cuban Intelligence, who drove us to a tiny apartment in which the space was confined to one bedroom with two beds and a small table, a small kitchen, and bathroom. It was here in this small Prague apartment where I really got to know this exceptional man. In the first two days I cleaned the apartment, made the coffee, boiled the water for his yerba mate, something he never gave up, and cooked light meals. Later we would take it in turns to do the work.

In the evenings we would sometimes go to a restaurant on the outskirts of Prague or for a drive around the city.

I'm always thinking about him, he regularly comes to mind … and I always see him reading, playing chess by himself, going over games from a book. Often he would challenge me to a game, insisting that I learn how to play until I had no option but to learn. I would win occasionally, at other times I would cheat. He was always asking why I didn't read. He would ask me to call him by the familiar "tú," to call him by his new name "Ramón" and he banned me from calling him Comandante. I found this really difficult, virtually impossible, until on one occasion he got so cross that he threw the book he had been reading to the floor. He was so upset that he told me never again to call him "Che" or "Comandante." Of course he was doing this for reasons of security, since there might have been bugging devices in the apartment and news of his being in Prague might slip out. Che was worried that he might be spotted and that his whereabouts would get back to the the CIA.

He had an amazing capacity to overcome illness. He exercised an almost unbelievable degree of self-control, something uncanny; and when he was unable to he got annoyed. He was an everyday fellow but a special one too thanks to his attributes and self-taught knowledge. I remember those difficult times when he would be suffering from an attack of asthma, especially because I too am a victim of that cruel affliction. When these occurred he would get hold of his equipment, some kind of little pump, and take his treatment. In spite of asthma he never gave up his tobacco! He would sit on the edge of his bed, having placed a chess board on a chair next to him; and now and then he would lift up his gaze and look at me to see if I was staring at him. Asthmatics have this tendency to not want people to look at them when they are having an attack.

He was a hard-working student, with a unique capacity for analysis and was very observant. He put what he learnt into practise, everything that he knew. When talking we would touch upon various topics: on one occasion I asked him about his beliefs and if he was already a communist before he met Fidel in Mexico. He told me that he hadn't been, at that time only having read and studied Marxist ideas, together with what he had witnessed during his trips to South America, Guatemala, and other countries where he had seen at first hand the hunger and suffering of the people. It had been Fidel who had been the definitive influence during their time in the Sierra Maestra, giving him plenty to read and then arguing and exchanging respective points of view. That was how he was to develop as a communist. His thoughts on racism were also very interesting. He assessed this from two differing perspectives, that of the person who discriminates and the person being discriminated against—native Americans, black or female. The person discriminated against does not know well enough how to stand up to the person discriminating against them.

His way of thinking was lateral. He was a man of few words: with a simple observation his opinion, his point of view were made very clear; and now and then his arguments would contain a special sense of humor and irony. As we spent so much time together in the small apartment it stood to reason that we would observe and be aware of each other's every characteristic. I remember once that Che was watching me smoking, staring at me then asking what country the cigarettes that I was smoking came from. I answered that they were North American. Jokingly, he said to me: "Couldn't you smoke less imperialist cigarettes?" Some time later I changed cigarette brands and, being as observant as he was, he again asked where they were from. This time I told him they were English. As soon as I told him that, with a little smile he replied: "Well, they're not as imperialist."

Some months later, and due to a security hitch, Che made the decision that I should return to Havana before him. The reason was due to my skin being black. In a city like Prague I attracted attention and there was the worry that we would be found out. In restaurants the waitresses would stare at me: they were fascinated by my black skin and my hair. So much so that when Che told me I had to leave he said: "Of course you'll be asking yourself why." And jokingly he added: "I've never seen a black man grab more attention than a white man." That's the way it was: because of the color of my skin and against the wishes of both of us I was unable to see my mission through to the end. I regretted it from the bottom of my heart as they were the most important months of my life.

Prague was a great experience for Che. He tried to get away from there by his own means … as he was already desperate to rejoin the fight. He even drew up a plan to get out on his own account with a couple of comrades. That was why Fidel had to send Osmany Cienfuegos and Ramiro Valdés to talk to him and persuade him not to. At the beginning of June 1966 Fidel wrote him a lengthy letter in which he set out the reasons for his return. First and foremost was the need for him to take part in the selection and training of the men who would set off to Bolivia with him. It was by these means alone that Fidel got Che to give up on the notion of leaving Prague on his own account. This letter has been published in *Pasajes de la Guerra Revolucionaria: Congo*.

Che would measure others as he measured himself and on occasions this would make him appear very harsh when weighing men up, in his assessment of his fellow combatants. However, on the other hand I acknowledge that there was only one Che Guevara. Every man, him included, has strengths and weaknesses and we all make mistakes. But what stands out about him is that his strengths are greater than his weaknesses, given that there is no such thing as the perfect man.

★ Preparing for Bolivia
In a revolution you either triumph or die

Che's mission to the Congo was as leader of a group of Cuban military advisers. Although all the Cubans were experienced in combat, it was never the intention for them to be incorporated into the rebel forces. The Congo was for Che a stepping stone towards his strategic goal of participating in a wider revolution in Latin America.

The journey back to Cuba was long and complicated as a result of the need to maintain secrecy. He spent long periods in the Cuban Embassy in **Dar-es-Salaam** and in a safe house in **Prague**. In Dar-es-Salaam he wrote up his **Congo diaries**. No personal record of his time in Prague has been released.

While in Dar-es-Salaam Che even found time to devote himself to planning a course of philosophy. In a letter to the Minister of Education, Amando Hart, he complained about the dreary tomes the Soviets were sending to Cuba which were "not only anti-Marxist but generally very bad." In a typically caustic aside he wrote that since the Revolution "we have already done much, but some day we are also going to have to think."

The man in charge of providing the logistical support from Havana for Che's international operations only gave his first interview about Che in 1997. According to Manuel Piñeiro ("Barba Roja," or Red Beard), far from being depressed following the failure of his mission to the Congo, Che was like "a boy with a new toy" when he returned to Cuba and began preparing for his Bolivia campaign in **Pinar del Río province**. He immersed his chosen group of guerrillas in rigorous physical and military preparation, including studying documents about Bolivia, classes in the native language Quechua, and mathematics.

After his return to Cuba Che saw his children only once, in his disguise as **Ramón** before leaving for Bolivia. The occasion must have been unbearably sad, as he could not reveal who he really was for fear that knowledge of his plans would leak out. Aleida introduced him to the children as a friend of their father. But he was able to see Aleida on several occasions. According to one source, Che was angry when a visit was arranged for Aleida to the training camp in Pinar del Río, because the wives of other fighters had not come as well.

Piñeiro states that Che selected Bolivia as his **center of guerrilla operations** in Latin America as "a training school for Latin American fighters which would permit the extension of the armed struggle to neighboring countries." In 1963 an attempt had been made to establish an Argentinian guerrilla base near the Bolivian border. A group of Peruvians, with Cuban support, attempted to establish a base on the Peruvian side of the border.

Che believed that if, from Bolivia, guerrilla columns could be formed with **fighters from various countries** of the southern cone, this would provoke a reaction from the governments of these countries, supported by US imperialism. That in turn would stimulate revolutionary armed struggle, which would lead the North Americans to intervene. "This would be another of the Vietnams which he called for in his historic Message to the peoples of the world through the Tricontinental organization."

Piñeiro believed that if Che's guerrilla base had not been discovered so early on by the Bolivian army, he might have succeeded in creating a substantial fighting force. "Knowing of the presence of Che in Bolivia, many cadres and fighters from various revolutionary forces on the continent would have found a way to come together and participate. The example of Che exercised a **great influence on many revolutionaries** within and beyond the borders of Latin America."

Let it be known that we have measured the extent of our actions and we consider ourselves as no more than elements within the great proletarian army

Left: **Preparing for Bolivia, Pinar del Río, 1966**

As soon as Che returned to Cuba from the Congo, he immediately began making preparations for launching a guerrilla campaign in Bolivia. The men who were to accompany him as volunteers were brought together at San Andrés in Cuba's westernmost province of Pinar del Río. This photograph was taken during training. It shows Che with his new disguised appearance, third from the right.

Day dedicated to Christmas Eve. Some people made two trips and arrived late, but we finally all got together and had a good time, with some people drinking too much.

Right: **Christmas dinner, Bolivia, 1966**

In their headquarters near the river Ñancahuazú, the guerrillas celebrated Christmas Eve in the traditional Cuban manner. Despite the difficult conditions, they were able to secure pork and alcoholic drinks. It was the last time Che and his comrades ate together in this way. From left to right: "Inti" (Guido Peredo, Bolivian); "Urbano" (Leonardo Tamayo, Cuban); "Rolando" (Eliseo Reyes, Cuban); "Fernando" (Ernesto Che Guevara); "Tuma" (Carlos Coello, Cuban); "Arturo" (René Martínez Tamayo, Cuban); and "el Moro" (Octavio de la Concepción de la Pedraja, Cuban).

It's one of those times when one has to take big decisions; this type of struggle affords us the chance to become revolutionaries, the highest stage of human development, and it also gives us the chance to graduate as men

Right: **The sentinel, Bolivia, 1967**

Whenever he could Che resumed his old habit of carefully recording his observations in his private diary. Although these notes were never intended for publication, they reveal a deeply sensitive observer, analytical and with a wry humor. Every tragedy, sadness and the occasional military victory are recorded meticulously over the 11 months of the campaign.

Left: **The traitor's children, Bolivia, February 1967**

While getting acquainted with the area where guerrilla operations were being mounted, Che visited the house of a peasant named Honorato Rojas, and provided medical assistance to his children, two of whom are seen here on his knee. Months later Rojas was to collaborate with the Bolivian Army in wiping out a group of Che's fighters.

★ Capture and execution

My country is much larger ... America is my country

At the beginning of October 1967, after 11 months of their Bolivian campaign, Che's guerrillas were sick and weak, reduced to 17 men and with **little chance of survival**. Informers reported their movements to the Bolivian army, and it could only be a matter of time before they were trapped.

By 7th October Che's band, having exchanged fire with the Bolivian soldiers some days before, were making their way through a ravine at 2,000 meters. The following day they were **trapped in a gulley**, their only chance of escape to fight their way out. In the battle that ensued Che was **hit by a bullet** in his left calf, and his carbine was put out of action by another bullet. Unarmed and vulnerable, he **tried to escape**, but was **captured** together with a Bolivian man named Simón Cuba ("Willy").

They were taken to the town of **La Higuera**. Che was questioned by the Bolivian Lieutenant Colonel Selich and, the next day, 9th October, by the CIA agent Felix Rodríguez, a Cuban émigré. In later accounts of both men Che remained **defiant**, confident that revolution would triumph in the Americas. A message arrived from the Bolivian High Command in La Paz **ordering Che's execution**. He was shot at 1:00 pm on 9th October.

Fearing the power of Che's example even in death, the army officers ordered that he and the other murdered guerrillas be **buried secretly**, although they announced that they had been cremated.

Thirty years later, Che's remains were found in a grave near **Vallegrande, Bolivia**. They were returned to Cuba and now rest in a mausoleum built in his honor, in the square of Santa Clara, the city he captured in the final battle of Cuba's revolutionary war.

Above: **José Angel Toirac, from the Gray series, the Heroic Guerrilla, oil on canvas, Guantanamo, Cuba, 2002**

And it must be said quite sincerely that in a true revolution, to which everything is given, from which no material returns are expected, the task of the revolutionary vanguard is both magnificent and anxious ... In these conditions, a great dose of humanity is needed, a sense of justice and truth, if we are not to fall in the trap of extreme dogmatism, of cold scholasticism or isolation from the masses. Every day you have to fight so that love for humanity can be transformed into concrete deeds, into acts that set an example, that mobilize.

Right: "We Will Be Like Che II," Department of Revolutionary Orientation archive, Havana

Last letter to his children (1965)

Dear Hildita, Aleidita, Camilo, Celia, and Ernesto,
If you ever have to read this letter, it will be because I am no longer with you.

Above all, always be capable of feeling deeply any injustice committed against anyone, anywhere in the world. This is the most beautiful quality in a revolutionary.

Until forever, my children. I still hope to see you. A great big kiss and a hug from

Papa

Above: **Che's son Camilo and daughter Celia, 1969**

Mass for the guerrilla

Father Javier Aruaga, head of the Missionary Team in the Americas, gave a lengthy sermon in memory of Che in the Temple of the Nazarenes, Lima, Peru. The priest related to his faithful how he had known the guerrilla leader in Cuba and that his death had moved him enormously.

"I was his friend," he said during the sermon. "And as such I have been profoundly affected by his physical departure."

He later added:

"During the time that I was living alongside Che, I tried to convince him that he should abandon his belief that God did not exist. But I could not. It was in the aftermath of the triumph of the Cuban revolution; and my role at the time was to take confession from those who had been sentenced to death. Guevara always said that social revolution required the use of arms as the pen may be mightier than the sword, but the sword brings victory. But contrary to what people may think, Che did not restrict himself to reading Marx, Engels or Lenin. He also read and studied Papal Encyclicals. Obviously, and as he never tired of saying, sermons and good intentions alone are not enough to achieve the liberation of the people."

Right: **"We Will Be Like Che I," Department of Revolutionary Orientation archive, Havana**

Above: **Photographs of Che's corpse, October 1967**

After Che's murder his Bolivian captors displayed photographs of his corpse on the walls of the town of Ñancahuazú.

Your light has not been quenched
Though you have fallen.
You move, guerrilla,
A figure on a flaming steed
Through the mountains, wind, and clouds,
Silenced, you are not silent.
And though they burn your body,
Though they hide you away
In graveyards, forests, cold uplands,
They cannot keep us from you
Che commander
Friend and brother.

Poem to Che by Nicolás Guillén,
15th October 1967

★ Che's burial
Return to Cuba, 1997

As a result of interviews conducted in Bolivia in 1995 by Jon Lee Anderson, a biographer of Che, the burial site of Che and six other murdered comrades was discovered. A team of Cuban archeologists and forensic experts began excavations in December 1995, and on 12th July 1997 formally identified Che's remains. The remains were returned to Cuba, and on 13th October a memorial ceremony was held in Revolution Square, Havana. The following day the remains were transferred to Santa Clara, where on 17th October a ceremony was held in the newly constructed mausoleum to Che, and a monument to Che by the sculptor Delarra was unveiled.

Right: Cortège with Che's remains leaves Revolution Square, Havana, for Santa Clara, 14th October 1997.

Following page: Aleida Guevara speaking in memory of her father, Che Guevara Mausoleum, Santa Clara, 17th October 1997.

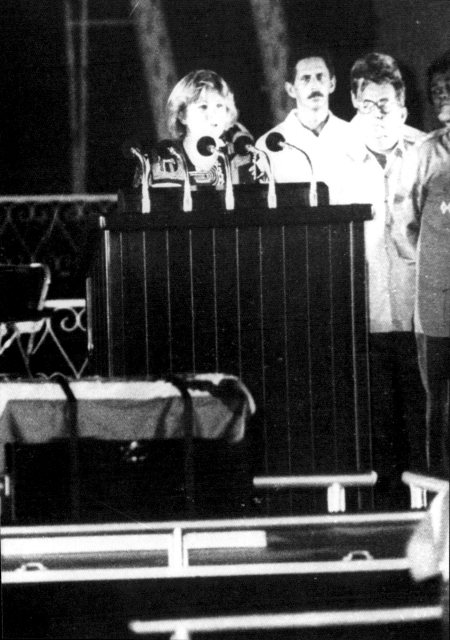

I have few memories of my father ... I think the most beautiful is of the day he saw us for the last time. We didn't know it was him, because he was disguised as the old Ramón. I was five and a half years old ... I banged my head on the table. He immediately took me in his arms ... I said to my mother, "Mamá, I have to tell you a secret. I think this man is in love with me."

Aleida Guevara, speaking about her father

Left: **Statue**

Monument to Che in the Che Guevara Revolution Square in Santa Clara, by the Cuban sculptor Delarra.

Legend

Chapter 5

The making of an icon

Che's life took on an epic quality which echoes the lives of great men throughout history. From his early youth he made long journeys, involved himself deeply in social problems, and threw himself into trying to change the world.

Shortly after Che's murder at the hands of the Bolivian army, his captors made a mask of his face and cut off his hands. They hoped that hard evidence of his death would diminish his legendary status. But mankind lives by its hopes and dreams, and Che's myth spread even faster with his martyrdom.

Despite his violent end, Che is not a tragic hero. Soon after photographs of his corpse were posted on the walls of the Bolivian town of Ñancahuazú, Che's image spread around the world as a symbol of hope for the oppressed, and of fear for their oppressors.

In 1968 the Italian publisher Feltrinelli made a poster from Alberto Korda's 1960 photograph. Millions of copies were sold and in no time left-wing movements had made Che their own.

Che's image has since been embraced by mainstream commerce. Che T-shirts, berets, and mousepads are everywhere, while rock stars, interior decorators, and fashion designers are constantly manipulating his famous face.

In Cuba, at first, this trend was resisted. But today even there the tourist shops are filled with souvenirs emblazoned with the image of the Heroic Guerrilla.

But Che's image is too poignant a symbol for commerce to have the last word. Artists in Cuba and the world have, since his

Previous page: **KEITH CARDWELL**, **Alberto Korda in his house with his photograph of the Heroic Guerilla, Havana, 1998**

death, paid homage to Che, and continue to rework his image in evocative paintings, photographs, and posters.

Che's self-sacrifice for a greater social good, and his timeless commitment to human values such as honor, truth, and loyalty continue to inspire the belief that the impossible can become the possible. Enigmatic, resolute, perhaps wistful, Che has entered the hearts and minds of millions.

Above: **HERIBERTO ECHEVARRÍA, Watercolor, 1968**

Above: **LUIS MARTÍNEZ PEDRO, "Che's America," Casa de las Américas collection, 1973**

8 Oct.

M
I
R

hasta la victoria siempre

Above: **HERIBERTO ECHEVARRÍA, 1980**

Above: **Volunteers, Havana, Prensa Latina, 1987**

Right: **Memorial service, Revolution Square, Havana, Prensa Latina, 18th October 1967**

Page 380: **Courtesy Department of Revolutionary Orientation archive, Havana**

Page 381 top: **Demonstration in Argentina, Prensa Latina, 1968**

Page 381 bottom: **La Higuera, Bolivia, Prensa Latina, 1969**

jornada del
guerrillero
heroico

octubre del 8 al 15

Above: SERGIO ROMERO, "The Icon," 1986

Above: **PERFECTO ROMERO, "Victory"**

Page 386: **Che Guevara camp, Cuba, Prensa Latina, 24th August 1970**

Page 387: **OLIVIO MARTÍNEZ, 1978**

Page 388: **PABLO LABAÑINO, 1978**

Page 389: **Revolution Square, Havana, 1967**

Page 390–1: **ISMAIL FRANCISCO, "Memory," 1970**

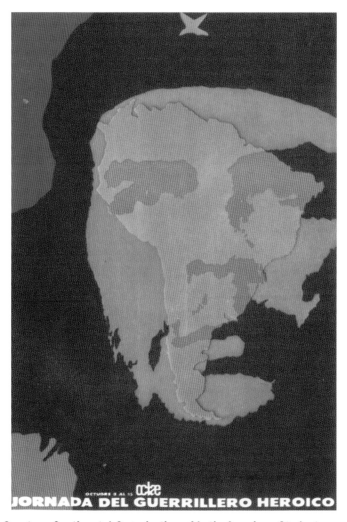

OCTUBRE 8 AL 15 oclae

JORNADA DEL GUERRILLERO HEROICO

Above: **Courtesy Continental Organization of Latin American Students
(OCLAE) archive**

CAMPAMENTO
CHE·GUEVARA
24·8·1970

8 de octubre/ October 8/ le 8 octobre   Día del Guerrillero Heroico ﻳﻮﻡ ﺍﻟﻤﻨﺎﺿﻞ ﺍﻟﺒﻄﻞ - ٨ ﺍﻛﺘﻮﺑﺮ
                                 Day of the Heroic Guerrilla
                                 Journée du Guérillero Héroique

OSPAAAL

Above: KEITH CARDWELL, "Falls Road, Belfast, Ireland," 2001

Right: ÑICO, **Department of Revolutionary Orientation archive, Havana, 1973**

Pages 394-5: KEITH CARDWELL, "Baracoa, Cuba"

Above: **Student demonstration, Santiago de Chile,
Prensa Latina, 1970**

Right: **ISMAEL FRANCISCO, 1st May 1997**

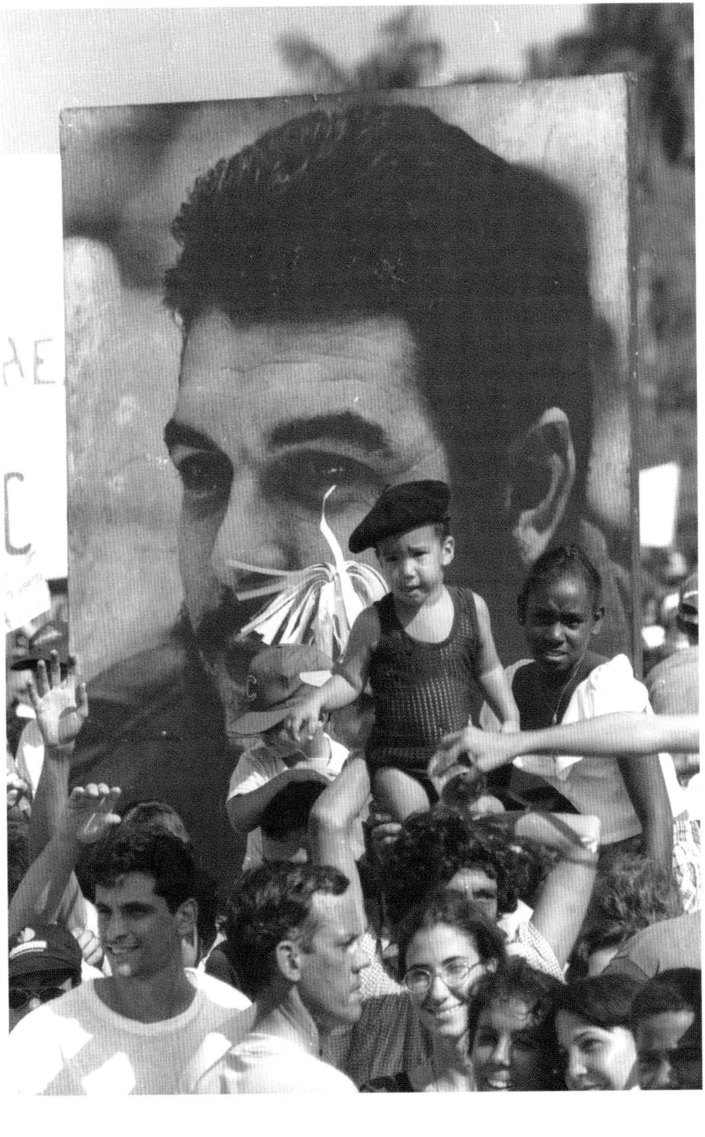

Above: **Peasant women, Bolivia, Prensa Latina, 1972**

Right top : GUILLERMO BELLO, **Cigarette pack**

Right middle : CHRISTIAN COUDURÈS, **Bottle of Prosecco wine from Italy**

Right bottom : **Canvas bag bearing the image of Che**

Above: **LISETTE SOLORZANO**

Right: **GUILLERMO BELLO**

Create two, three, many Vietnams

In January 1966, following a conference in Havana, an organization was established to foster support for struggles against imperialist domination of the nations of the Third World—the Organization of Solidarity with the Peoples of Asia, Africa, and Latin America (OSPAAAL). Although Che was not present at the conference—he had left Cuba in April of the previous year to fight in the Congo—OSPAAAL answered directly to his central preoccupation, the need to develop the economic and political independence of the oppressed nations.

OSPAAAL established its own magazine, *Tricontinental*. Its first edition, published on 16th April 1967, contained a message from Che which became known throughout the world in the years that followed. It was titled "Create two, three, many Vietnams," and it called "for the unity of the peoples against the great enemy of the human race: the United States of North America." This, in effect, became Che's last will and testament.

Che argued that the "miserable peace" that followed the end of World War Two was bought at the cost of the "poverty, degradation, constantly increasing exploitation of enormous sectors of humanity." But even this peace was punctuated by imperialist wars, notably in Korea and Vietnam.

Che foresaw that the fight of the Vietnamese against the half-million-strong US invasion force would lead to the defeat of US imperialism, and he upheld it as an inspiration to oppressed peoples everywhere.

Right: **VOTTA, Cover, Tricontinental magazine, OSPAAAL**

TRI¹³⁸continental

ISSN 0564-1590

30 YEARS OF LIBERATING
COMMUNICATION

EXCLUSIVE
COMANDANTE ERNESTO
CONVERSATION WITH COMMANDER

Above: RAFAEL ENRÍQUEZ, Cover, Tricontinental magazine, OSPAAAL

Above: **Cover, Tricontinental magazine, OSPAAAL**

Above: **Cover, Tricontinental magazine, OSPAAAL**

Above: **RAFAEL ENRÍQUEZ, Cover, Tricontinental magazine, OSPAAAL, 1980**

Above: **RAFAEL ENRÍQUEZ, Cover, Tricontinental magazine, OSPAAAL, 1985**

Above: **GLADYS ACOSTA, Cover,**
Tricontinental magazine, 1991

Above: **ELENA SERRANO, Cover,**
Tricontinental magazine, 1968

Above: **ORLANDO YANEZ, Cover,**
Tricontinental magazine, 1977

Above: **PABLO LABAÑINO, Cover,**
Tricontinental magazine, 1975

Above: RENÉ MEDEROS, Cover, Tricontinental magazine

Above: **A poster for the Organization for Solidarity among the Peoples of Asia, Africa, and Latin America (OSPAAAL)**

Above: **RAFAEL ENRÍQUEZ, 1982**

Above: **VICTOR MANUEL NAVARETTE, 1976**

Above: **Courtesy Department of Revolutionary Orientation archive, Havana**

Above: **ALBERTO BLANCO, 1990**

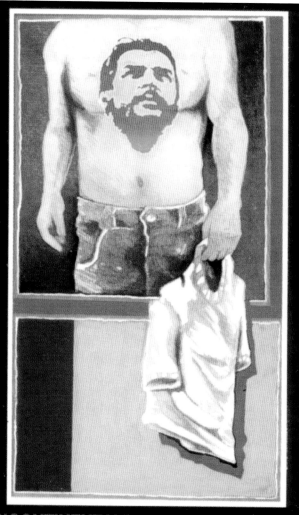

"TRICONTINENTAL" ΕΛΛΗΝΙΚΗ ΕΚΔΟΣΗ

410

Η επίσημη έκθεση που έγινε στην Αβάνα για την επέτειο των 30 χρόνων από την δολοφονία του Τσε.

Above: **Cover, Tricontinental magazine. The Greek title reads "Che Guevara."**

Left: **Cover, Tricontinental magazine**

Above and Right: RENÉ MEDEROS, from the series of silk screen prints of Che

Left and Above: RENÉ MEDEROS, from the series of silk screen prints of Che

Map of Cuba following Che's trail

Che's headquarters pre- and post-1959, and his route from the Sierra Maestra to the Escambray mountains

La Cabaña

El Taburete

San Andrés

LA HABANA

MATANZAS

PINAR DEL RIO

SANTA CLARA

Isla de Pinos

Pedrero

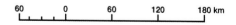

60   0   60   120   180 km

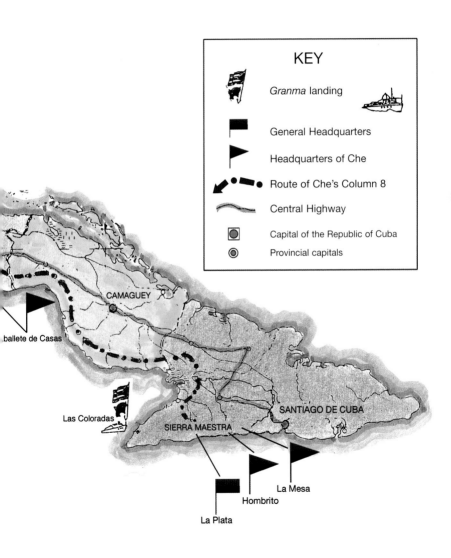

KEY

Granma landing

General Headquarters

Headquarters of Che

Route of Che's Column 8

Central Highway

Capital of the Republic of Cuba

Provincial capitals

CAMAGUEY

ballete de Casas

Las Coloradas

SANTIAGO DE CUBA

SIERRA MAESTRA

La Mesa

Hombrito

La Plata

Photo Credits

Photographers

© **Perfecto Romero:** pages 48, 106, 115, 116, 120, 122, 125, 126, 129, 131, 138–139, 145, 146, 146a, 147, 149, 153, 158, 162, 174, 175, 188, 199, 202, 206, 216, 218, 224, 231, 244, 249, 260, 317, 324, 384

© **Rogelio Andrés Torres:** pages 74–75, 108, 112, 150, 154, 178, 179, 183, 187, 214, 215, 255, 270, 271, 282, 297, 301

© **Liborio Noval:** pages 205, 222, 223, 226, 227, 238, 242, 256, 259, 266, 267, 298, 302

© **Eliseo de La Campa from Perfecto Romero personal Archive:** pages 280, 281, 304, 306

© **Chino López:** pages 5, 250, 296

© **Lisette Solorzano:** page 400

© **Guillermo Bello:** pages 399, 401

© **Sergio Romero:** pages 382–383

© **Keith Cardwell:** pages 372–3, 392, 394–5

© **Ismail Francisco:** pages 390, 397

© **Christian Coudures:** page 399

Archives

Office of Historical Affairs of the Council of State: pages 12–13, 18, 18a, 19, 20, 21, 22, 23, 24, 26, 27, 28, 30, 30a, 31, 32, 33, 37, 38, 39, 41, 42, 44, 46, 60, 63, 64, 65, 66, 68, 71, 73, 78, 79, 80, 82, 85, 86, 88, 89, 90, 92, 92a, 93, 93a, 94, 97, 98, 102, 103, 110, 134, 135, 136, 137, 157, 160, 166, 168, 170, 171, 172, 173, 173a, 177, 184, 185, 200, 201, 201a, 208, 210, 211, 213, 220, 228, 233, 234, 240, 246, 247, 248, 254, 272, 275, 276, 278, 284, 285, 286, 290, 292, 294, 295, 300, 308–309, 319, 320, 323, 332, 335, 336, 339, 348, 351, 353, 354

Prensa Latina: pages 252, 268, 288, 367, 368, 370, 378, 379, 381, 386, 396

Courtesy Organization for Solidarity with the People of Asia, Africa and Latin America (OSPAAAL): pages 2, 8–9, 55, 101, 243, 303, 313, 340, 403–405, 408

Courtesy Ulises Estrada: pages 377, 387, 388, 393, 403, 404, 405, 405a, 405b, 405c, 405d, 406, 407, 408, 409a, 409b, 409c, 409d, 410, 411, 412, 413, 414, 415

Courtesy Casa de Las Américas: pages 133, 142, 331

Courtesy Continental Organization of Latin American Students (OCLAE Archive): page 385

Courtesy Che Guevara Center: page 119

Courtesy Cuban Department of Revolutionary Orientation Archive: pages 359, 361, 363, 380

Courtesy Mirtha Ibarra: pages 191, 192, 193, 193a, 194, 196

Heriberto Echeverría: pages 79, 181a (stamp), 375

José Angel Toirac: page 357

Quotation Credits

Note: Original references have been used wherever possible, usually taken from Cuban editions. In all cases references have been left in the original language, in all editions of this book.

Chapter One Child, student, traveler

p14: Ernesto Che Guevara, *Notas de Viaje*, Editorial Abril, 1993, p18

p16: Ernesto Che Guevara, *Notas de Viaje*, Editorial Abril, 1993, p56

p17: Ernesto Che Guevara, *Notas de Viaje*, Editorial Abril, 1993, p108

p20: Ernesto Guevara Lynch, *Mi Hijo el Che*, Editorial Arte y Literatura, 1988, p176

p27: Ernesto Guevara Lynch, *Mi Hijo el Che*, Editorial Arte y Literatura 1988, p 214–215

p29: *Poemas del Che*, Instituto Cubano del Libro, 1969, p17

p31: John Gerassi (ed.), *Venceremos! The speeches and writings of Che Guevara*, Panther Books, London, 1969, p29

p32: Ernesto Che Guevara, *Notas de Viaje*, Editorial Abril, 1993, p17

p34: Ernesto Che Guevara, *Notas de Viaje*, Editorial Abril, 1993, p18

p35: Compilación Escritos y Discursos, *El Che en la Revolución Cubana*, Ministerio del Azúcar, Tomo II, Discurso pronunciado Acto de Inauguración de un ciclo de Charlas Ministerio Salud Publica, 19 de agosto 1960, p304

p36: Adys Cupull y Froilán González, *Cálida Presencia, Evocación Tita Infante*, Editorial Oriente, p102

p38: Jesús Soto Acosta, *Che: una vida, un ejemplo*, Colección 100 Años de Lucha, Editora Política, 1968, p25

p40: Andrés Castillo, Exclusive interview with Alberto Granado, *The Che Handbook*, MQ Publications 2003

p42: Ernesto Che Guevara, *América latina, Despertar de un continente*, Ocean Press, 2003, p29

p43: Alberto Granado, *Un largo viaje en moto de Argentina a Venezuela*, Cuba, Período Granma, 17 de octubre 1967

p45: Ernesto Che Guevara, *Notas de Viaje*, Editorial Abril, 1993, p18

p47: Ernesto Che Guevara, *Notas de Viaje*, Editorial Abril, 1993, p24

p56: Ernesto Che Guevara, Una revolución que comienza, *Obras Escogidas 1957–1967*, Tomo I, Casa de las Américas, 1970, p193

p58: Hilda Gadea, *Che Guevara años decisivos*, Ediciones Aguilar, México, 1972, p56

p61: Ernesto Che Guevara, Pasajes de la Guerra Revolucionaria: El Patojo, *Obras Escogidas 1957–1967*, Tomo I, Casa de las Américas, 1970, p431

p62: Ernesto Che Guevara (inéditos), *Otra vez*, Editorial Abril, 2000, p73

p65: *Memoria*, De los viaje: Segunda Mirada a América Latina, Centro Cultural Pablo de la Torriente Brau, Ediciones Unión 1998, p14

p67: Telma Bornot Pujillones, *De Tuxpan a la Plata*, Editorial Orbe, Habana, 1979, p67

p69: Ernesto Che Guevara, Una revolución que comienza, *Obras Escogidas 1957–1967*, Tomo I, Casa de las Américas, 1970, p193

p70: Ernesto Che Guevara, Una revolución que comienza, *Obras Escogidas 1957–1967*, Tomo I, Casa de las Américas, 1970, p192

p72: Ernesto Che Guevara, Una revolución que comienza, *Obras Escogidas 1957–1967*, Tomo I, Casa de las Américas, 1970, p195

Chapter Two Guerrilla fighter

p76: Ernesto Che Guevara, Una revolución que comienza, *Obras Escogidas 1957–1967*, Tomo I, Casa de las Américas, 1970, p196

p83: Ernesto Che Guevara, Pasajes de la Guerra revolucionaria, *Obras Escogidas 1957–1967*, Tomo I, Casa de las Américas, 1970, p11

p84: Ernesto Che Guevara, La Guerra de Guerrillas, *Obras Escogidas 1957–1967*, Tomo I, Casa de las Américas, 1970, p110

p87: Compilación Escritos y Discursos, *El Che en La Revolución Cubana*, Combate de Arroyo del Infierno, Ministerio del Azúcar, Tomo VII, p226

p88: Paco Ignacio Taibo II, *Ernesto Guevara más conocido por el Che*, Editorial Joaquín Mortiz, Grupo Editorial Planeta, México, 1996, p145

p91: Ernesto Che Guevara, Pasajes de la Guerra revolucionaria, Alegría de Pío, *Obras Escogidas 1957–1967*, Tomo I, Casa de las Américas 1970, p200

p94: Compilación Escritos y Discursos, *El Che en la Revolución Cubana*, Discurso Sociedad Nuestro Tiempo, enero 1959, Ministerio del Azúcar, Tomo II, p11

p96: Ernesto Che Guevara, Pasajes de la Guerra revolucionaria, *Obras Escogidas 1957–1967*, Tomo I, Casa de las Américas 1970, p343

p99: Ernesto Guevara Lynch, *Mi Hijo el Che*, Editorial Arte y Literatura, 1988, p21

p100: Ernesto Che Guevara, Pasajes de la Guerra revolucionaria, *Obras Escogidas 1957–1967*, Tomo I, Casa de las Américas, 1970, p291

p102: Ernesto Che Guevara (inéditos), *Otra vez*, Editorial Abril, 2000, p73

p104: Ernesto Che Guevara, Pasajes de la Guerra revolucionaria, *Obras Escogidas 1957–1967*, Tomo I Casa de las Américas, 1970, p400

p105: Ernesto Che Guevara, Pasajes de la Guerra revolucionaria, *Obras Escogidas 1957–1967*, Tomo I, Casa de las Américas, 1970, p401

p107: Ernesto Che Guevara, Pasajes de la Guerra Revolucionaria, *Obras Escogidas 1957–1967*, Tomo I, Casa de las Américas, 1970, p404

p109: *América Latina despertar de un continente, Qué cubano nos parece el mundo*, Ocean Press, 2003, p198

p111: Ernesto Che Guevara, *Algo Nuevo en América*, Sesión de Apertura Primer Congreso Latinoamericano de Juventudes 28 julio 196, Editora Abril, 2001, p42

p112: Antonio Núñez Jimenez, *El Che en Combate*, Ediciones Mecgraphic Ltda, La Habana Cuba 1996, p192

p114: Ernesto Che Guevara, Pasajes de la Guerra Revolucionaria, La ofensiva final, *Obras Escogidas 1957–1967*, Tomo I, Casa de las Américas 1970, p407

p117: Ernesto Che Guevara, *Escritos y Discursos*, Tomo I, Editorial Ciencias Sociales, Habana, 1972, p131

p118: Ernesto Che Guevara, Pasajes de la Guerra revolucionaria, La ofensiva final, *Obras Escogidas 1957–1967*, Tomo I, Casa de las Américas 1970, p409

p121: Ernesto Che Guevara, *América Latina, despertar de un continente*, Poesía inédita, "A los Mineros de Bolivia," Ocean Press, 2003, p136

p123: Antonio Núñez Jimenez, *El Che en Combate*, Ediciones Mecgraphic Ltda., La Habana Cuba, 1996, p192

p124: *Revista Bohemia*, Febrero, 1959

p127: *Life* Magazine, Enero, 1959

p128: *Revista Bohemia*, Poesía Ernesto Che Guevara, Poema "Oda a Fidel," junio 1988, p131

p131: Compilación Escritos y Discursos, *El Che en la Revolución Cubana*, Historias de la Revolución: Camilo, Ministerio del Azúcar, Tomo I, p340

p132: Compilación Escritos y Discursos, *El Che en la Revolución Cubana*, Historias de la Revolución:Camilo, Ministerio del Azúcar, Tomo I, p343

p134: Ernesto Guevara Lynch, *Mi hijo el Che*, Editorial Arte y Literatura, La Habana 1988, p90

p136: Ernesto Guevara Lynch, *Mi hijo el Che*, Editorial Arte y Literatura, La Habana 1988, p.90

p137: *Memoria*, Centro Cultural Pablo de la Torriente Brau, La Piedra, Ediciones Unión, 1998, p23

Chapter Three Statesman, ambassador, husband, father

p140: Compilación Escritos y Discursos, *El Che en la Revolución Cubana*, Carta 11 Noviembre 1962, Ministerio del Azúcar, Tomo I, p411

p143: Compilación Escritos y Discursos, *El Che en la Revolución Cubana*, Acto en su honor, 20 Enero 1959, Ministerio del Azúcar, Tomo II, p 2

p144: Compilación Escritos y Discursos, *El Che en la Revolución Cubana*, Discurso, Semana de Liberación de Santa Clara, 5 Enero 1960, Ministerio del Azúcar, Tomo II, p144

p151: Compilación Escritos y Discursos, *El Che en la Revolución Cubana*, Discurso en la entrega de Premios a trabajadores destacados en la Emulación Socialista, Ministerio del Azúcar, Tomo V, p253

p152: Compilación Escritos y Discursos, *El Che en la Revolución Cubana*, Natalicio de Martí Ministerio del Azúcar, Tomo II, p162 p155: Compilación Escritos y Discursos, *El Che en la Revolución Cubana*, Cartas, 11 de noviembre, Ministerio del Azúcar, Tomo I, 1963, p431

p161: Compilación Escritos y Discursos, *El Che en la Revolución Cubana*, Pasajes de la Guerra Revolucionaria, Cuidando a los heridos, Ministerio del Azúcar, Tomo VII, p301

p169: Ernesto Guevara Lynch, *Mi hijo el Che*, Editorial Arte y Literatura, Habana, 1988, p428

p170: Compilación Escritos y Discursos, *El Che en la Revolución Cubana*, La India país de grandes Contrastes, Ministerio del Azúcar, Tomo I, p11

p171: *Memoria*, La palabra entrevista, América Latina, Centro Cultural Pablo de la Torriente Brau, Ediciones Unión, 1998, p17

p174: Compilación Escritos y Discursos, *El Che en la Revolución Cubana*, Programa de TV Ante la Nación, 14 Diciembre, 1964, Ministerio del Azúcar, Tomo V, p340

p175: Compilación Escritos y Discursos, *El Che en la Revolución Cubana*, Programa de TV Ante la Nación, 14 Diciembre, 1964, Ministerio del Azúcar, Tomo V, p346

p176: Ernesto Che Guevara, Discurso en Conmemoración del II Aniversario de Integración de las Organizaciones Juveniles, *Obras Escogidas 1957–1967*, Tomo II, Casa de las Américas, 1970, p173

p180: Compilación Escritos y Discursos, *El Che en la Revolución Cubana*, Ante la Prensa: Ciclo de Conferencias en el Banco Nacional, 20 Octubre 1960, Ministerio del Azúcar, Tomo II, p368

p182: Compilación Escritos y Discursos, *El Che en la Revolución Cubana*, Ceremonia de Premiación a un grupo de trabajadores ganadores de la emulación, 31 de enero 1962, Ministerio del Azúcar, Tomo IV, p79

p184: *Memoria*, La palabra entrevista, América Latina, Centro Cultural Pablo de la TorrienteBrau, Ediciones Unión, 1998, p15

p186: Ernesto Che Guevara, *Che Guevara habla a la Juventud*, Sesión de apertura al Primer Congreso Latinoamericano de Juventudes, Editorial Pathfinder, USA, 2000, p42

p189: *Memoria*, La palabra entrevista, América Latina, Centro Cultural Pablo de la Torriente Brau, Ediciones Unión, 1998, p17

p190: Silvia Oroz, *Tomás Gutiérrez Alea: Los Filmes que no filmé*, Ediciones Unión, 1989, pp45, 49

p200: Ernesto Che Guevara, Carta a su hija Hildita, *Obras Escogidas 1957–1967*, Tomo II, Casa de las Américas, 1970, p694

p203: Ernesto Che Guevara, Carta a María Rosario Guevara, 20 de febrero 1964, *Obras Escogidas 1957–1967*, Tomo II, Casa de las Américas 1970, p 685

p204: Compilación Escritos y Discursos, *El Che en la Revolución Cubana*, Programa de TV Ante la Nación, 14 Diciembre, 1964, Ministerio del Azúcar, Tomo V, p339

p207: Ernesto Che Guevara, Discurso, Conferencia Mundial de Comercio y Desarrollo, Ginebra 25 Marzo 1964, *Obras Escogidas 1957–1967*, Casa de las Américas, 1970, Tomo II, p208 p210: Compilación Escritos y Discursos, *El Che en la Revolución Cubana*, Entrevista para el Sovetskaya Rossia, 2 de noviembre 1960, Ministerio del Azúcar, Tomo II, p414

p211: Compilación Escritos y Discursos, *El Che en la Revolución Cubana*, Conferencia Televisiva, 6 de Enero 1961, Ministerio del Azúcar, Tomo III, p16

p212: Ernesto Guevara, Discurso en la Conferencia Mundial de Comercio y Desarrollo en Ginebra, Marzo 1964, *Obras Escogidas 1957–1967*, Casa de Las Américas 1970, Tomo II, p540

p217: Antonio Núñez Jimenez, *En Marcha con Fidel*, Letras Cubanas, Havana, 1982, p231

p219: Compilación Escritos y Discursos, *El Che en la Revolución Cubana*, Inauguración de la Fábrica de Bujías, 17 Mayo 1964, Ministerio del Azúcar, Tomo V, p157

p221: Ernesto Che Guevara, El Socialismo y el Hombre en Cuba, *Obras Escogidas 1957–1967*, Tomo II, Casa de las Américas, 1970, p372

p222: Compilación Escritos y Discursos, *El Che en la Revolución Cubana*, Discursos, Entrega de Certificados de trabajo Comunista, 15 Agosto 1964, Ministerio del Azúcar, Tomo V, p217

p225: Compilación Escritos y Discursos, *El Che en la Revolución Cubana* Discurso en el auditórium de la Universidad central de las Villas, 28 de diciembre 1959 Ministerio del Azúcar Tomo II, p139

p229: *Time* Magazine, 8 August 1960

p230: Ernesto Che Guevara, *América Latina despertar de un continente*, Selección de Cartas, 1953–1956, Carta a sus padres, México julio 1956, Ocean Press, 2003, p161

p232: Ernesto Che Guevara, Discurso en Punta del Este, Uruguay, Conferencia del Consejo Interamericano Económico y Social de la OEA, *Obras Escogidas 1957–1967*, Tomo II, Casa de las Américas, 1970, p424

p239: Compilación Escritos y Discursos, *El Che en la Revolución Cubana*, Soberanía e Independencia Política, 20 de Marzo 1969, Ministerio del Azúcar, Tomo II, p217

p245: Paco Ignacio Taibo II, *Ernesto Guevara también conocido como el Che*, Editorial Joaquín Mortiz, Grupo Editorial Planeta, México, 1996, p488

p246: Compilación Escritos y Discursos, *El Che en la Revolución Cubana*, Discurso a los funcionarios y empleados del Ministerio de Industrias, 6 de Octubre 1961, Ministerio del Azúcar, Tomo III, p465

p248: Compilación Escritos y Discursos, *El Che en la Revolución Cubana*, Discurso en la sesión de Apertura del Primer Congreso latinoamericano de Juventudes, 28 de Julio 1960, Ministerio del Azúcar, Tomo II, p301

p251: Ernesto Che Guevara, *América Latina, despertar de un continente*, Carta a su madre, México 15 de julio 1956, Ocean Press, 2003, p160

p253: Compilación Escritos y Discursos, *El Che en la Revolución Cubana*, Clausura del seminario La Juventud y la Revolución, 10 Mayo 1964, Ministerio del Azúcar, Tomo V, p151

p257: Compilación Escritos y Discursos, *El Che en la Revolución Cubana*, Clausura del Primer Encuentro Internacional de Profesores y Estudiantes de Arquitectura 29 Septiembre 1963, Ministerio del Azúcar, Tomo IV, p505

p258: *Memoria*, La palabra entrevista, América Latina, Centro Cultural Pablo de la Torriente Brau, Ediciones Unión, 1998, p17

p266: Ernesto Che Guevara, El Socialismo y el hombre en Cuba, *Obras Escogidas 1957–1967*, Casa de Las Américas, Tomo II, p374

p270: *Revista Prisma*, Severo Nieto, Pasión por el deporte, Febrero, 1987

p271: *El Mundo*, Comentarios del Maestro Eleazar Jiménez, 23 de agosto 1963

p273: Compilación Escritos y Discursos, *El Che en la Revolución Cubana*, Discurso en el auditórium de la Universidad central de las Villas, 28 de diciembre 1959 Ministerio del Azúcar Tomo II, p 138

p274: Compilación Escritos y Discursos, *El Che en la Revolución Cubana*, Entrevista sección Siquiatrilla, 11 de noviembre 1963, Ministerio del Azúcar, Tomo IV, p519

p279: Compilación Escritos y Discursos, *El Che en la Revolución Cubana*, Ciclo de Conferencias en Salud Pública, 19 de Agosto 1960, Ministerio del Azúcar, Tomo II, p306

p281: Ernesto Che Guevara, El Socialismo y el Hombre en Cuba, *Obras Escogidas 1957–1967*, Tomo II, Casa de las Américas, 1970, p382

p283: Compilación Escritos y Discursos, *El Che en la Revolución Cubana*, Reporte Ministerial 1961–1962; Autocrítica y sugerencias críticas, Ministerio del Azúcar, Tomo VI, p705

p284: Compilación Escritos y Discursos, *El Che en la Revolución Cubana*, Entrevista Jean Daniel en Argel, 25 de Julio 1963, Ministerio del Azúcar, Tomo IV, p465

p285: Compilación Escritos y Discursos, *El Che en la Revolución Cubana*, Entrevista para publicaciones argelinas, 16 de abril 1964, Ministerio del Azúcar, Tomo V, p129

p286: Ernesto Che Guevara, Mensaje a los Pueblos del Mundo en la Conferencia Tricontinental, *Obras Escogidas 1957–1967*, Tomo II, p586

p289: Compilación Escritos y Discursos, *El Che en la Revolución Cubana*, Entrevistas con Estudiantes norteamericanos que visitaron Cuba, Ministerio del Azúcar, Tomo IV, p479

p292: Compilación Escritos y Discursos, *El Che en la Revolución Cubana*, Inauguración de la Planta Mecánica "Fabrica Aguilar Noriega" en Santa Clara, 5 de mayo 1964, Ministerio del Azúcar, Tomo V, p414

p293: Ernesto Che Guevara, XIX Periodo de Sesiones de la Asamblea General de Naciones Unidas, Derecho de réplica, *Obras Escogidas 1957–1967*, Casa de las Américas, Tomo II, p561

p295: Ernesto Che Guevara, XIX Discurso ante la Asamblea General de Naciones Unidas, *Obras Escogidas 1957-1967*, Casa de las Américas, Tomo II, p541

p296: Ernesto Che Guevara, Segundo Aniversario de la Integración de organizaciones juveniles, *Obras Escogidas 1957–1967*, Casa de las Américas, Tomo II, p174

p300: Compilación Escritos y Discursos, *El Che en la Revolución Cubana*, Un pecado de la revolución, Ministerio del Azúcar, Tomo I, p345

p305: Edición especial dedicada al Che Guevara, con prólogo de Haydée Santamaría, *Revista Casa de las Américas*, febrero 1986, p90

p310: Ernesto Che Guevara, Carta de despedida a sus hijos, *Obras Escogidas 1957–1967*, Casa de las Américas, Tomo II, p696

Chapter Four International fighter

p312: Ernesto Che Guevara, Carta de despedida a Fidel, *Obras Escogidas 1957–1967*, Tomo II, Casa de las Américas, p693

p314: Ernesto Che Guevara, *Obras Escogidas 1957–1967*, Tomo II, Casa de las Américas, p697

p318: *Memoria*, Carta a sus hijos, Escribo desde muy lejos, América Latina, Centro Cultural Pablo de la Torriente Brau, Ediciones Unión, octubre 1998, p21

p321: Ernesto Che Guevara, *Pasajes de la Guerra revolucionaria, Segundo Acto*, Editorial Grijalbo Mondadori, 1999, p44

p322: *Memoria*, La Piedra, Centro Cultural Pablo de la Torriente Brau, Ediciones Unión, Octubre, 1998, p23

p334: Ernesto Che Guevara, *Pasajes de la Guerra revolucionaria, El Congo*, Epílogo, Editorial Grijalbo Mondadori, 1999, p332

p338: Ernesto Che Guevara, *Pasajes de la Guerra revolucionaria, El Congo*, Epílogo, Editorial Grijalbo Mondadori, 1999, p334

p346: Ernesto Che Guevara, Carta de despedida a Fidel, *Obras Escogidas 1957–1967*, Tomo II, Casa de las Américas, p697

p349: Ernesto Che Guevara, Mensaje a los pueblos en la Conferencia Tricontinental, Suplemento especial 16 abril 1967, *Obras Escogidas 1957–1967*, Casa de las Américas, Tomo II, p98

p350: Ernesto Che Guevara, *Diario en Bolivia*, Editora Política, Habana, 1987, p42

p352: Ernesto Che Guevara, *Diario en Bolivia*, Editora Política, Habana, 1987, p30

p356: *Memoria*, De la Guerra, Eduardo Galeano, Centro Cultural Pablo de la Torriente Brau, Ediciones Unión, octubre 1998, p17

p358: Ernesto Che Guevara, El Hombre y el Socialismo en Cuba, *Obras Escogidas 1957–1967*, Casa de las Américas, 1967, Tomo II, p382

p360: Ernesto Che Guevara, Carta del Che a sus hijos, *Obras Escogidas 1957–1967*, Casa de las Américas, 1967, Tomo II, p696

p362: *Diario Así*, Misa por el Guerrillero, 27 Octubre, 1967

p365: *Poesía, Nicolás Guillen*, Che comandante, amigo, Editorial Letras Cubanas, Havana, 1997

p371: Aleida Guevara March, Ese hombre está enamorado de mí, *Juventud Rebelde*, La Habana, octubre 1997

Bibliography

Che Guevara left behind a large collection of diaries, letters, speeches, essays, and books. Many of the speeches have still not been published outside Cuba, but the most important writings are available in a number of languages. One of the best selections is *Che Guevara Reader: writings on guerrilla strategy, politics & revolution*, (Ocean Press, 1997) which contains an extensive bibliography of published works by Che.

Among Che's most important published writings are: *Pasajes de la Guerra revolucionaria (Episodes of the Revolutionary War);La Guerra de Guerrillas (Guerrilla Warfare); Notas de Viaje (The Motorcycle Diaries)* on his youthful journey around South America; *Diario del Che en Bolivia (Bolivian Diary)*; and *Pasajes de la Guerra Revolucionaria: el Congo* (not translated).

There are many memoirs by people who knew Che. Of particular interest are, by his father Ernesto Guevara Lynch, *Mi Hijo el Che* (Editorial Arte, Havana, 1988); and *Che: a memoir by Fidel Castro* (Ocean Press, 1994).

Thirty years after his death, three massive biographies of Che appeared, two by Mexicans and one by a North American. The first was Paco Ignacio Taibo II's *Ernesto Guevara: también conocido como el Che* (Planeta, 1996, translated as *Guevara, also known as Che*, St. Martin's Press, 1997). This was followed by Jon Lee Anderson's *Che Guevara: a revolutionary life* (Bantam Books, 1997) and Jorge Castañeda's *La vida en rojo* (Alfaguara, 1997). All three are based on extensive research and, with their often contrasting viewpoints, make fascinating reading.

Index

Page references in *italics* refer to illustration captions

www.stmartins.com

ISBN 0-312-32246-1

First published in Great Britain by MQ Publications.

First U.S. Edition: October 2003

10 9 8 7 6 5 4 3 2 1

Printed in China

8th Jan	Fidel Castro arrives in Havana.
17th May	First agrarian reform law is proclaimed.
2nd June	Che and Aleida March marry.
12th June	Che sets out on a long trip through Europe, Africa, and Asia to negotiate commercial and technical agreements, returning 8th September.
7th Oct	Che appointed head of industrial department of the National Institute of Agrarian Reform.
26th Nov	Che appointed president of the National Bank.

★ 1960

4th Mar	*La Coubre*, a French ship carrying Belgian arms, explodes in Havana harbor as a result of sabotage, killing 81 people.
29th June	Revolutionary government nationalizes US oil refineries when they refuse to refine Soviet oil.
9th July	Soviet Union agrees to purchase all Cuban sugar that the United States refuses to buy.
6th Aug	Major US companies nationalized.
19th Oct	United States imposes partial trade embargo on Cuba.
21st Oct	Che leaves for two-month trip that takes him to the Soviet Union, East Germany, Czechoslovakia, China, and North Korea.
24th Nov	Che and Aleida's first child, Aleidita, is born.

★ 1961

3rd Jan	The United States breaks diplomatic relations with Cuba.
23rd Feb	Ministry of Industry established, with Che as Minister.
17th Apr	1,500 Cuban émigré mercenaries with US backing invade Cuba at the Bay of Pigs on the south coast to the west of Cienfuegos, but are defeated within three days at the battle of Playa Girón.
8th Aug	Che speaks at the conference of the Organization of American States in Punta del Este, Uruguay, as leader of the Cuban delegation.

★ 1962

3rd Feb	President Kennedy imposes total trade embargo of Cuba.
20th May	Che and Aleida's son Camilo is born.
27th Aug	Che visits the Soviet Union.
22nd Oct	President Kennedy denounces Cuba's acquisition of nuclear missiles and imposes a naval blockade on the island.
28th Oct	Soviet Prime Minister Khruschev brings the "Cuban Missile Crisis" to an end by agreeing to remove its missiles from Cuba in exchange for the United States removing its missiles from Turkey and pledging not to invade Cuba.

★ 1963

14th June	Che and Aleida's daughter Celia is born.